Jehovah's Witnesses hate Jehovah

Bruce Benson

Heart Wish Books

Jehovah's Witnesses hate Jehovah

Published by Heart Wish Books
Cambridge, Massachusetts

heartwishbooks@gmail.com

All Bible quotations are the author's paraphrase
unless marked

Scripture quotations marked (KJV) are from

the King James Version in the public domain

ISBN: 978-0999803905

Library of Congress Control Number: 2020903434

Religion – Christianity – Apologetics
Religion – Blasphemy, Heresy and Apostasy

Contents

Chapter four ... Did Jesus say He is God? 4

Chapter five ... Who is the Jehovah's Witnesses' father?

Chapter six ... The Son of man

How are Jesus and Jehovah one?

"Me and Jehovah are one" - Jesus, John 10:30

Only Jesus

Is the Holy Spirit a person?

Chapter ten ... Conclusion

This is for you, Karlos,
to ease your pain.
I know what the Jehovah's Witnesses
have done to you.

Rest assured,
God will punish them.
And He will stand by you,
the true man of God.

I pray that the Word of God
explained in this book
will lead your loved one
to the true Jesus of the Bible
and to salvation.

Chapter One

Introduction

Here's what happened:
First, I studied the Bible on my own for a number of years. Then I did a street ministry in Harvard Square, in Cambridge, Massachusetts, for seven years — from 2009 to 2016 — using homemade Bible quiz questions and pamphlets. I wrote a book, AHA moments from the Bible, about the encounters I had in Harvard Square, and the questions people asked me, and how I answered them.

I left Harvard Square and did the same ministry at an intersection in Boston called Downtown Crossing. And every day at Downtown Crossing I saw at least two groups of Jehovah's Witnesses with their displays. So, I decided to look into the Jehovah's Witnesses' teachings.

It's a battle for people's souls
Jude wrote that Christians must <u>earnestly contend</u> for the Christian faith because there are always impostors sneaking in and pretending to be Christians. A lot of people <u>can't see</u> that they're pretending because they disguise themselves. Jude said they pervert the grace of God, and that they deny our <u>Lord</u>, Jesus Christ.   (Jude 1:3-4)

In the original Greek, the words <u>earnestly contend</u> that Jude used, are just one word. It's epagonizomai. It's where we get the English word agonize. It means a strenuous battle. The Greeks used it to refer to athletic competition and for warfare on a <u>battlefield</u>.

I didn't pick a fight with the Jehovah's Witnesses. They started this fight. I'm fighting back to defend the truth and to fight for people's souls. The Jehovah's Witnesses are <u>enemies</u> of Jesus Christ. Jude is telling Christians that we are to strenuously do battle against the enemies of Jesus Christ. That's why I wrote this book.

Do you want an overpolished university book, written by an intellectual snob? No, of course you don't. This book comes from real life, from my experiences on the street. This flows through my veins. And I'm doing this for the love.

The same old enemies of Jesus

The Jehovah's Witnesses have some things in common with the Pharisees, the enemies of Jesus when He walked the earth.

> They both deny that Jesus is God. They both reject God's indwelling Holy Spirit. And both of them put their followers into bondage to man-made rules and regulations.

I'm going to focus on one thing. And that is the Jehovah's Witnesses' teaching about who Jesus is. Naturally, that will include who the Holy Spirit is.

Here's what the Jehovah's Witnesses teach:

• They teach that Jesus was the first thing that God created, and that then Jesus created everything else. And, the Jehovah's Witnesses teach that Jesus is the archangel Michael.

• They teach that the Holy Spirit is not a person.

How do I know the Jehovah's Witnesses teach those things?

You can go to the Jehovah's Witnesses' website and see for yourself that they teach those things. It's called JW.org.

The Jehovah's Witnesses' Jesus is a freak, a Frankenstein monster. There's no such animal. The Jehovah's Witnesses' Jesus walks and talks like he's God, <u>but</u>, they say, he is <u>not</u> God.

You're either God or you're not

There's no such thing as a 75% God alongside a 100% God. There's not God and a semi-God. The Jehovah's Witnesses' Jesus is zero percent God, and that makes their Jesus a loser, a cheap imitation.

> The idea that Jesus is not God is so evil that it could only have come from the imagination of the devil.

The Jehovah's Witnesses are building on a bad foundation. The fall of their house will be great.

(Luke 6:47-49; 1 Corinthians 3:9-11)

What's the big deal?

I once told a man that the Jehovah's Witnesses teach that Jesus is not God. And he said, "What's the big deal?"

The big deal is this: <u>God</u> is our Savior. So, a Jesus who is less than 100% God can't save anybody, meaning he can't get anyone into Heaven, he can't give anyone eternal life, he can't save anyone from God's anger and vengeance because of our <u>sins</u>. He's an impostor sent by the devil to trick people. That's why the idea that Jesus is not God is the most offensive, deadliest, biggest big lie of all time.   (See Romans 1:18)

To say that Jesus is not God is to do away with the Christian faith.

We <u>sin</u> when we break God's laws found in the Bible: 1 John 3:4.

"I, yes I, am God, and there is no savior besides Me"

- God, Isaiah 43:11

> One time at my street ministry, a woman told me she'd been a
> Jehovah's Witness for thirty-five years. Then she asked me, "Why do
> you think Jesus is God?" My answer? "For the same reason I think
> there are fish in the ocean."

The apostle John wrote an account of the life of Jesus. We call it the
Gospel of John. And at the end of his Gospel, John wrote:

"There are many other things that Jesus did, which, if every one of
them were written about, I think the whole world would not be big
enough to fit all the books that they would fill.

And Jesus did many things that were out-of-this-world, things that
His disciples saw Him do, which are not written in this book.

But these specific things were written. Why? So that when you read
them you can believe that Jesus is the Christ, the Son of God. And so
that by believing in Him you can have eternal life."

John 20:30-31; 21:25

I'll show you how to study the Bible correctly

Then you'll be able to see that when John said that Jesus is the Christ,
the Son of God, what John meant is that Jesus is God. And when John
said that you can have eternal life by believing in Jesus, he meant that
Jesus is God the Savior.

And I think the whole world could not contain all the books that could
be written to prove from the Bible that Jesus is God. But I will show
you more than enough in this small book for you to see that Jesus is
God, as easily as you can see that there are fish in the ocean. And it will
be more than enough for you to see that Jesus is your Savior.

"Ask, and it will be given to you, seek, and you will find,
knock, and it will be opened to you."

- Jesus, Matthew 7:7

Who is our Guide?

The Jehovah's Witnesses are clever. They pass themselves off as just regular Christians. They might tell you they believe that Jesus is God. But when they say "God," what they mean is "god." Or they might tell you they believe that Jesus is the Son of God. But remember, they teach that God created Jesus. That's not the Son of God of the Bible. The Son of God of the Bible is God.

They will try to confuse you by showing you passages in the Bible that could make you think that Jesus is not God. It's when you show only one side of the evidence in order to mislead someone.
That's called lying.

But I'm going to introduce you to someone. If you will let them, they will be your Guide. When you start to get worried or confused then you can look to the Guide and they will keep you on the right path.

Your Guide is the knowledge that Jesus is God. That knowledge is found over and over throughout the Bible. That knowledge will be our Foundation, our Guide, our Light, our Rock, and our Fortress.

I will show you the Guide as we go on. Here's one to get you started:

"In Jesus dwells all the fullness of Godhead bodily."
Colossians 2:9

The word Godhead means God. This verse is saying that God came and walked among us in a human body. This verse states clearly that Jesus Christ is 100% God. That's our Guide.

And our Guide will be there for us, to comfort us, over and over.

"Your Word is a lamp to my feet, and a light to my path."
Psalms 119:105

"Jehovah" is the word the "Jehovah's Witnesses" use for the sacred name of God found in the original Hebrew of Exodus 3:14. So, in order to make my point more clearly, in some Bible verses where the words "God," "Lord," or "the Father" appear, I will use the word "Jehovah" instead.

When I say "Jehovah's Witnesses hate Jehovah" it's like saying, "Bob's employees hate Bob."

Jehovah said this:

"You are My <u>witnesses,</u> and My servant that I have chosen,
so that you will know and believe Me, and understand
that I am He who is.

There is no such thing as a god that
was created before Me or after Me.

I am Jehovah, and there is no savior besides Me."

- Jehovah, Isaiah 43:10-11

The Jehovah's Witnesses claim that <u>they</u> are the witnesses for Jehovah that He spoke of in that passage. But that's a lie, because the Jehovah's Witnesses hate Jehovah.

I say it because Jesus said it:

> "Whoever hates Me hates Jehovah too."
>   - Jesus, John 15:23

For many years the Jehovah's Witnesses have been hunting down Jesus like dogs chasing a rabbit. They show their hatred for Jesus by telling lies about Him, by saying that Jesus was the first thing Jehovah created. They belittle Jesus and drag His good name through the mud when they call Him "a god."

The Jehovah's Witnesses insult Jesus and cheapen His reputation when they say that Jesus is the archangel Michael.

> They're like the Roman soldiers who mocked Jesus, punched Him, spit in His face and stripped off His clothing. The Jehovah's Witnesses strip Jesus of His position as God.   (Matthew 26:67; 27:27-31)

And Jesus said that whoever hates Him hates Jehovah too. That's why the title of this book is, "Jehovah's Witnesses hate Jehovah."

I guess it's irony, or sarcasm.

If you're not a Christian but you're seeking, then read this book, and use it to get started on your own journey of Bible study.

Will you see the truth? That's between you and God. It's something that will happen in the quiet place in your mind. If it doesn't happen right away, then be patient, don't quit.

> One day you could be walking down the street or you could be at work or talking to someone, and God could open your heart and your mind and give you the truth about Jesus, just like God did for Lydia.
> (See Acts 16:14-15)

At the end of AHA moments from the Bible I said I was working on a second book, about deception. But because of the urgent need, I decided to do this part of that book first, separately.

I wrote, edited, and designed this book by myself over the winter of 2019 to 2020. I'm an ordinary person, not a professional writer or a professional theologian. This is a homemade, self-published book, for those who love truth.

This book could have been bigger, but I made it smaller on purpose. That will make people more likely to want to read it. There are more examples I could have given in each section, but I gave enough.

You have to do your part
Don't go by what I say. You have to do your <u>own</u> enthusiastic studying to show God that you're seeking the truth earnestly. As you read my book you should have a Bible open next to you. I've provided many Bible verses that you can look up, read, and study on your own.

If you don't know how to study the Bible or if you don't know where the books of the Bible are, then this book can help you get started. Maybe one day you too will be a defender of the faith.

And if you already are a defender of the faith, I hope my book helps you.

I said on the back cover that I'd show you clues that God placed in the Bible which prove that Jesus is 100% God and that you cannot go to Heaven if you believe in a Jesus who is anything less than 100% God.

I'm sure I've given you clues that I'm not aware of. Maybe you'll see them. Let me know what you find. If the only thing that happens to you as a result of reading this book is that it gets you to open your Bible, then it's done its job.

The best thing you could do for me is to give me something I can use. Tell me what you agree with or what you don't agree with.

Bruce Benson   heartwishbooks@gmail.com

Chapter two

Are you a Greek scholar?

Here's what the apostle John wrote:

> "The Word was God."   John 1:1

Jesus is the Word. And here's our Guide again. Our Guide is the clear statement in the Bible that Jesus always was God, and always will be God. Even the Jehovah's Witnesses couldn't deny that John 1:1 clearly states that Jesus is God. They had a problem. They dealt with it by writing their own so-called Bible. And in their Bible, John 1:1 says "the Word was a god," instead of "the Word was God."

How could they call Jesus "a god"?

Okay, ready? In the original Greek version of the words "the Word was God," the word "the" does not appear before the word "God." Therefore, the Jehovah's Witnesses conclude that instead of saying "God," it should say, "a god," and therefore Jesus is not "God" but "a god." Does your head hurt now? Mine too. But don't worry, I'm going to make it all better in a minute.

Did you understand that? The bit about the Greek word for "the" not being before the word "God"? No, of course you didn't, not if you're like me and know nothing about the rules for constructing sentences in Greek.

> You might find someone who is a "Greek scholar" who agrees with the Jehovah's Witnesses that this passage should be translated "the word was a god." They might be lurking in some dark corner somewhere. But you won't find a credible Greek scholar or Bible translation that agrees with the Jehovah's Witnesses.

I won't bore you by including a Greek grammar lesson or the long list of Greek scholars who say that the lack of the word "the" does not change the fact that the correct translation is, "the Word was God." You can google that if you like. Thank you for not falling asleep. Now I'm going to reward you for your patience with a wonderful truth.

Can <u>we</u> understand the Bible?

You might be thinking, what hope do <u>we</u> have of understanding the Bible? Those of us who aren't Greek scholars. My dear reader, you don't think our loving Heavenly Father would give us a Bible that could only be understood by Greek scholars, do you? Here's the wonderful truth that I promised would make it all better:

The apostle Peter did not have a degree in Greek from a Bible school. But Peter knew the truth.

One day, Jesus said to His apostles:

> "I have a question for you: Who am I?"   Matthew 16:15

The apostle Peter spoke up and said:

> "You are the Christ, the Son of the living God." Matthew 16:16

Now maybe Jesus said, "Peter! Shut your mouth! You have no right to say such a thing. You're an uneducated fisherman, not a Greek scholar!"   (See Acts 4:13)

No, Jesus didn't say that. Jesus said this:

> "Be very happy Peter, because you were not told who I am by a man. It was My Father, God in Heaven, who let you know who I am."
> Matthew 16:17

Jesus said Peter wasn't just parroting what he'd been told by a man like people in cults do. Jesus said <u>God</u> gave Peter that knowledge about who Jesus is.   (See Luke 10:21)

If God gives you the truth, then you'll know more than Greek scholars stacked a mile high. Study your Bible and ask God to teach you like He taught Peter. The best Greek scholar in the world won't know the truth if God doesn't give them the truth. Never let anyone tell you that you can't understand the Bible because you're not a Greek scholar.

What steps should I take?

There are steps a person needs to take in order to understand a passage in the Bible. Here are three of them:

First, study the meaning of the words in the languages they were written, the Hebrew and Greek. Really? Yes. Get yourself a Strong's Concordance. Then look around for books that show you what the English words meant in the languages they were originally written, the Hebrew and Greek. Thank God for Hebrew and Greek scholars!

Second, study the context in which the passage was written. What was said before and after the passage? Who was speaking and who were they speaking to? What does it mean to the person it was spoken to and what does it mean to us? What does the passage mean in the context of the Bible as a whole?

Third, what does your God-given understanding tell you that the passage means?

> To understand what a passage in the Bible means, you always have to let context trump word meanings. The meaning of some words change according to the context in which they're used. And God-given understanding is king.

These three steps are for those who diligently study their Bible and who have been given God's Holy Spirit. The Jehovah's Witnesses might be diligently studying the Bible, but they are lost, they will never see the truth. Why? Because they say that the Holy Spirit is not a person.

> God wrote us a book, the Bible. He used words. But the words alone will not reveal to us the truths God is telling us. We have to go deeper than the words. The only way we will see the deeper truths in the words is when God reveals them to us by His Holy Spirit.

Chapter three

I want to start with these

A father sends his son off to war in order to preserve peace and safety in America. But the son never returns, he dies in battle. It grips your heart, you sob uncontrollably. It's unbearable. But the father and son did that out of love. Love of country, love of family and fellow citizens, and love of God. Why? Because freedom doesn't just happen. Freedom is costly. Because of the sacrifice made by millions we are still free in America to worship God.

> What I've just described is something we can understand. And that's what God is trying to get us to understand about why Jesus is called the Son of God

God's Son died to give people freedom from sin, from death, and from the devil.   (Hebrews 2:14-15)

"God did not spare His own Son, but delivered Him up for all of us."
Romans 8:32

The definition of sin is the breaking of God's laws found in the Bible. Breaking God's laws brings misery and death. God showed us how serious sin is, and how much He loves us, by painting a picture of a father losing his son. And God showed us how serious sin is by telling us in the Bible what Jesus went through to pay for our sins.
(Matthew 27:27-31; 1 John 3:4)

This is the most famous verse in the Bible:

"God loves all the people of the world so much, that He gave the life of His only begotten Son, Jesus, so that anyone who believes in Jesus will not perish, but will have everlasting life."   John 3:16

> To help us understand John 3:16, God gave us Genesis 22:1-19, written almost two thousand years before John 3:16 was written.

"Thanks be to God for the gift He gave us, a gift which cannot be fully explained in words."   2 Corinthians 9:15

Does that make you picture an old man with a white beard sitting next to a young man? I'm going to show you why that's all wrong.

• In Matthew 26:64, Jesus said that the Son of man will sit <u>at</u> the <u>right hand</u> of God.

The word <u>at</u> was translated into English from the Greek word <u>ek</u>. It's #1537 in the Strong's Greek dictionary. <u>Ek</u> means <u>out from</u>.

Jesus said this:
"The Father feels affection for you because you love Me, and you believe the truth, that I <u>came out from God</u>." John 16:27

And in the Bible, the expression, "right hand" is used symbolically to refer to a person's power, actions, and creativity.   (Numbers 9:23)

• Hebrews 1:3 says that when Jesus finished His mission as the humble Son of man, God lifted Jesus up to the highest place: He sat down <u>at</u> the right hand of God, back to where He came out from.
                                                                (See John 17:5)

In Hebrews 1:3, the word <u>at</u> was translated into English from the Greek word <u>en</u>. In this verse <u>en</u> means the energy inside a person that comes out into the world and does things. En is #1722 in Strong's.

God used an expression we can understand, "sitting at someone's right hand." No one except Jesus "sits at God's right hand." It proves that Jesus is God Himself who came out from God and lived among us. Jesus is not a second person sitting next to Jehovah.

God is Spirit. God can't come to earth as He is. So, God <u>comes out from</u> Himself and comes to earth in whatever form He wants. Jesus is Jehovah stepping out of Himself to do whatever He wants. (John 4:24)

The apostle John wrote:

"Jesus was in the beginning with God."   John 1:2

A passage in the Book of Proverbs is the key to understanding what is meant by Jesus being <u>with God</u>. The Bible interprets itself!

In Proverbs we find someone who tells us that they too were with God in the beginning. Her name is Wisdom. She tells us that she was beside God when He created everything. She too already existed in the beginning. And it was by her that God formed the earth.
                    (Proverbs 3:13,18-19; 8:1-3; 22-30; See Psalms 33:6; John 1:3)

Wisdom is a woman. Does that mean God is a woman? No. Jesus once compared Himself to a hen, but Jesus is <u>not</u> a chicken.
                    (Matthew 23:37; See Exodus 19:4; Psalms 17:8)

> If Wisdom was <u>with</u> God in the beginning, then who is Wisdom?
> Is she a second person? Another God? A god? No, she's none of those.
> Writers sometimes make a thing speak as though the thing is a person.
> It's done to make their writing come alive, make it more enjoyable to
> read, and easier to understand.

<u>Wisdom is a thing</u>. In Proverbs, a thing, wisdom, is speaking to us as though she is a person. That's <u>God's</u> wisdom. God gave her a name, Wisdom, called her "her," and had her speak to us. So, when she says she was "with God," she wasn't a second person. She was, and is God's wisdom. So, she <u>is</u> God, 100% God. Simple, right?

<u>Words are a thing</u>. God spoke of His words as though words are a person. But God outdid what He did in Proverbs with His wisdom. God's words actually became a person, with flesh, blood, and bones. So, when John says that Jesus was <u>with God</u>, he doesn't mean that Jesus was a second person. Jesus is God's words. Jesus is God, 100% God.

"And the Word was made flesh"   John 1:14 (KJV)

Chapter four

Did Jesus say He was God?

Has anyone ever told you that Jesus never said He was God? They're wrong. Of course Jesus said He was God. That's why the people wanted to kill Jesus — because He said He was God. That's why Jesus was sentenced to death — because He said He was God. That's why they punched Jesus, spit in His face, and nailed Him to a cross to die — because He said He was God. I'll show you.

In John 5:17, Jesus said:

"My Father works constantly, and I am also working." - Jesus

What happened when Jesus said that?
When the people heard Jesus say that, they wanted to kill Him. They knew what Jesus meant. Their law said that anyone who said what Jesus said must be sentenced to death.

(John 5:18; See Deuteronomy 13:1-11)

> If a human being has a son, then that son is 100% human, right? Well, if God has a Son, then that Son is 100% God. That's what Jesus meant when He said, "My Father works constantly, and I work." He was saying that God was His own Father. Jesus was making Himself equal with God. He was saying that He is 100% God.

What if you don't understand what Jesus said?
Even if you can't understand what Jesus meant in John 5:17, you can see that what I'm saying is true. How? Well, the people wanted to kill Jesus because He made Himself equal to God by calling God His own Father. Jesus knew that, even if they didn't say it. Jesus knows what people are thinking.

> Did Jesus apologize? Did He say they misunderstood Him? No, He did not. So, yes, Jesus _did_ say that He is God.

Why does it say "the Jews"?
You might have noticed that I changed John 5:18. It says "the Jews" wanted to kill Jesus, but I changed it to "the people" wanted to kill Jesus. I did that because evil people have spread the lie that "the Jews killed Jesus."

Who are the "Jews" then in John 5:18? Jesus told us in Revelation 2:9 and 3:9. They are evil people pretending to be Jews. Just like there are evil people pretending to be Christians.

No genuine Jewish person would have murdered Jesus.

One time, Jesus told His apostles to get in a boat and go across the sea to a town named Bethsaida. Jesus didn't go with them. Instead, Jesus went by Himself to a mountain so He could pray.

Sometime between 3 and 6 in the morning the apostles were struggling to row the boat against strong winds. At the same time, Jesus was walking on the sea, and would have walked right by them. The apostles didn't know it was Jesus. They thought it was a ghost. But they were so scared they cried out for help anyway.

When Jesus heard their cry, He said to them, "Don't worry, I am. Don't be afraid." And Peter said, "If You are I am, then command me to walk to You on the water." So, Peter got out of the boat and walked on the water. But when Peter took his eyes off Jesus and remembered the wind, he started sinking.

Jesus reached out His hand and caught Peter. Then Peter and Jesus got in the boat and the wind stopped. The apostles were amazed beyond measure as they thought about what had just happened. They worshiped Jesus, and said to Him, "You truly are the Son of God."
(See Matthew 14:22-33; Mark 6:45-54)

In my Bible, Jesus says, "It is I," not, "I am."
That's why we need Bible study books. There's one called an Interlinear Bible. It shows you the Bible in English, along with the original Hebrew and Greek. That way you can see a whole sentence in the original languages.

Look at Matthew 14:27 or Mark 6:50, where it's reported that Jesus said, "It is I." In an Interlinear Bible you'll see that what Jesus said is, "Ego eimi." What's that? That's the words "I am" in Greek.

Jesus comforted the apostles by saying, "Don't worry, I am." When Moses asked Jehovah, "What is Your name?" Jehovah said, "My name is I am." (See Exodus 3:14)

Jesus referred to Himself as "I am" many times. The people were familiar with Exodus 3:14 and they knew precisely what Jesus meant. One time, Jesus said this to the people

> "Truly, truly, I say to you, Before Abraham was, I am."
> - Jesus, John 8:58

When the people heard Jesus say that, they picked up stones to stone Him to death. But Jesus hid Himself and walked right through them and went on His way.   (See Deuteronomy 13:1-11)

> The people knew that when Jesus said He was "I am," He was saying that He is God. And that was a death penalty offense. Jesus knew it was a death penalty offense. But, Jesus could say He was "I am" because it's true. Jesus told the truth but they killed Him.

The power of God
Later on, some evil men came to arrest Jesus on false charges. Jesus said to them, "Who are you looking for?" They said, "We're looking for Jesus of Nazareth." And Jesus said, "I am." As soon as Jesus said "I am," all of those evil men fell backwards to the ground.

(John 18:3-6)

And Jesus said this:

> "If you do not believe that I am, then you will die in your sins."
> - Jesus, John 8:24

> The Jehovah's Witnesses do not believe that Jesus is I am.

In Mark chapter 14, beginning at verse 53, we read that after Jesus was arrested on false charges by the so-called religious authorities, He was brought before <u>their</u> high priest.

The high priest asked Jesus,
   "Are You the Christ, the Son of <u>the Blessed</u>?"   Mark 14:61

And Jesus said,
   "<u>I am</u>, and you will see the Son of man sitting at the right hand of <u>Power</u>. And I'll be coming back here with the armies of Heaven."
                              - Jesus, Mark 14:62

When the high priest asked Jesus if He was "the Son of the Blessed," he meant "the Son of God." And when Jesus said He would be sitting "at the right hand of Power" He meant at God's right hand.
                                        (See Psalms 110:1)

Jesus said He was God when He said that He was the Christ, the Son of the Blessed, and when He said He would be sitting at God's right hand, and when He said He would be coming back as the Judge.
                                        (See Daniel 7:13-14)

And there's one other way that Jesus said He was God. When the high priest asked Him if He was the Son of the Blessed, Jesus answered, "I am" (Ego eimi in Greek). God said to Moses, "Tell the children of Israel that I am has sent you."   (Exodus 3:14)

Yes, Jesus was saying that He is I am. Yes, Jesus said He was God's own Son. Yes, Jesus said He is God. So, they accused Jesus of speaking evil against God and sentenced Him to death. They thought they were obeying Leviticus 24:16. But they were wrong because Jesus <u>is</u> God.
                                        (Mark 14:64)

   "We have a law, and according to the law He has to die, because He made Himself God's own Son."   John 19:7   (See Leviticus 24:16)

One day, Jesus and His disciples were walking through the corn fields. His disciples were hungry, so they started picking and eating the corn.
(Matthew 12:1)

That was perfectly legal according to the law of Israel. A hungry person could pick and eat corn in a stranger's corn field as long as they didn't carry any corn out of the field.   (See Deuteronomy 23:25)

The Pharisees gave Jesus a hard time again
The Pharisees weren't complaining that the disciples were eating the corn. They accused the disciples of disobeying the law that said no one was allowed to do any <u>work</u> on the sabbath day, the day God ordered to be set aside as a day of rest. The Pharisees were claiming that the act of picking and shucking the corn was work that was not permitted on the sabbath day.   (Matthew 12:2; See Exodus 20:8-11)

Jesus told the Pharisees that when they saw His disciples lawfully eating the corn, they should have shown them mercy, and not condemned the innocent.   (Matthew 12:7; See Hosea 6:6)

Jesus reminded the Pharisees that the priests in God's temple have to work on the sabbath day so they can serve God. And that when David was starving, he went into the temple and ate holy bread that only priests were supposed to eat.   (See Leviticus 24:5-9; 1 Samuel 21:1-6)

.   (Matthew 12:3-5)

And Jesus said this to the Pharisees:
   "There is someone here who is greater than the temple."
                                   - Jesus, Matthew 12:6

The temple was the place where the children of Israel worshiped God. And here is Jesus saying that He is greater than the temple.

Then Jesus said this:

   "The Son of man is Lord of the sabbath."
                                   - Jesus, Matthew 12:8

So, the Pharisees set a trap

When the Pharisees heard Jesus say that, they got an idea. They wanted to make Jesus look bad so the people wouldn't leave them and go and follow Jesus. So they brought a man to Jesus. The man had lost the use of his hand.

They asked Jesus, "According to the law of Israel is it lawful to heal a person on the sabbath day?" They were hoping that if Jesus said, "Yes," then they could accuse Jesus of going against the law and then Jesus would be condemned by the people.

But Jesus asked them if there was any among them who, if they owned only one sheep, and their sheep fell into a pit on the sabbath day, would leave the sheep in the pit and not pull it out.

Jesus also said, how much more valuable is a person than a sheep? And Jesus concluded that therefore it is lawful to do a good deed on the sabbath day. Then Jesus healed the man's hand.

That was it for the Pharisees. They went off and had a meeting to plan how to destroy Jesus.   (Matthew 12:9-14)

Only someone who is God Himself could say that they are greater than the temple and are Lord of the sabbath day. When Jesus said those things He was clearly stating that He is the God of the Old Testament, that He is Jehovah.

Jesus was found guilty of death by the high priest. But only the Roman government could carry out a legal execution. So Jesus was taken to the Roman governor Pontius Pilate. Jesus knew that Pilate had the authority to sentence Him to death.   (Mark 14:63-64; John 18:31)

In 1 Timothy 6:13, the apostle Paul encouraged Timothy by reminding him that Jesus testified honestly and agreed with what Pilate said.

Paul was talking about what happened in Matthew, chapter 27, beginning at verse 11. Pilate asked Jesus, "Are You the King of the Jews?" The King James Version says that Jesus answered, "Thou sayest." It's an expression, like when someone says, "You got that right." It means Jesus answered Pilate's question by saying "Yes."

Jesus knew that by answering "Yes" it would cost Him His life. You can read John's report of this incident and know for sure that Jesus answered "Yes" (See John 18:37).

Who is the King of the Jews? God is.

"Jehovah is our Judge, Jehovah is our Lawgiver, Jehovah is our King: He will save us."   Isaiah 33:22

When Jesus called Himself the King, did the people say, "All hail the King"? No they yelled, "Crucify Him!" Why? Because they understood that when Jesus said He was the King of the Jews, that Jesus was saying that He is God.   (Matthew 27:21-31)

When Jesus told the people that He is God, Jesus wasn't telling the people to worship a false god. Jesus told the truth when He said He is God. But the people killed Him anyway. The people thought they were obeying Deuteronomy 13:1-11, but they were wrong because Jesus is God.

In Israel there was a tax that everyone had to pay in order to support the temple. Some officials came from the temple to ask Peter if Jesus had been paying that tax. Peter said, "Yes." (Matthew 17:24-25)

Jesus was staying at Peter's house and when Peter got home Jesus asked him a question. Jesus said, "Tell Me what you think Peter: Who do the kings of the earth take taxes from? Do they take them from their own children or from the children of other families?" Peter said, "They take taxes from the children of other families." (Matthew 17:26)

And Jesus said, "Then the children of the king are free from being taxed. But even though that's true, we don't want to offend them. So, do this: Go to the sea and cast a hook. Take the first fish you catch and open its mouth. You'll find a coin in its mouth. Take it and give it to the temple officials. It will be enough to pay the tax for Me and for you also." (Matthew 17:26-27)

So, where am I going with this? First, what did Jesus call the temple? In John 2:16 Jesus called the temple, "My Father's house." And Jesus told Peter that the children of the earthly king are free, that the king does not take taxes from them.

> Jesus used that example about human kings to teach Peter that Jesus is the Child of God, the King. Only Jesus is the Child of God the King in that way.

Then why did Jesus pay the tax for Peter too? Jesus didn't pay for any of the other apostles. Why only Peter? Well, when you stay at someone's house it's only right to do something to help them out.

Did you notice something in the last two examples I just gave? Jesus is both the King and the Child of the King.

Jesus is called "King" in Psalm 2:6, and "Son" in Psalm 2:7. Compare Isaiah 9:6 with Luke 2:11. Read the story Jesus told in Matthew 22:1-15.

Chapter five

Who is the Jehovah's Witnesses' father?

Who is the Jehovah's Witnesses' father?

Jesus told us who the Jehovah's Witnesses' father is:

> "If Jehovah was your Father then you would love Me because I came out from and went forth from My Father, Jehovah. I did not come from Myself, but Jehovah sent Me.
>
> Do you know why you won't believe in Me? It's because you can't understand what I'm saying. And you can't understand what I'm saying because you came from your father, the devil, and you want the same things that your father wants.
>
> The devil was a murderer from the beginning, and he refused to stand for the truth because there is no truth in him.
>
> The devil is a liar. In fact, he's the father of lies. And when the devil speaks lies he's speaking to his own children.
>
> The reason why you refuse to believe in Me is because I speak the truth."
>
> - Jesus, John 8:42-45

Who is a liar?

The apostle John wrote:

> "Who is a liar? Whoever says that Jesus is not the Christ is a liar. They have the spirit of the <u>Antichrist</u> because they reject Jehovah and the Son. Because whoever rejects the Son does not have Jehovah."
> 1 John 2:22-23

Who is the Antichrist?

You can read about the Antichrist in 2 Thessalonians 2:8-9. He's called "the lawless one." He is the devil. He will dazzle people by performing what appear to be miracles. But they are a lie.

The answer is in 2 Thessalonians 2:10-12. The Antichrist can trick them into accepting his lie because they don't love the truth. So, God lets the Antichrist give them a convincing fraud, and they believe a fraud instead of the truth. They wouldn't take pleasure in God's saving truth. Now they take pleasure in a lie instead.

(See Zechariah 7:11-13; 2 Timothy 4:3-4)

> You can't reject the Son and have Jehovah. You can't have one without the other. Whoever denies the Son is denying Jehovah. That's the spirit of Antichrist.

The truth is simple for those who want to see it. But what does the devil do to those who choose not to see? The Bible calls the devil "the god of this world," and says that the devil blinds the minds of those who refuse to believe, and hides the truth about Jesus from them.

(2 Corinthians 4:3-4)

Who is a murderer?

Jesus said that the devil was a murderer from the beginning. And, just like their father, the Jehovah's Witnesses are murderers of people's souls. They can't kill a person's soul, only God can do that. But the devil and the Jehovah's Witnesses give people a lie, a false gospel which leads them to a spiritual death. (Matthew 10:28)

The true "Gospel" is the Good News that Jesus Christ, God Himself in a flesh body, lived a sinless life, gave His life as a sacrifice for our sins, then rose from the dead, and is now in Heaven. And anyone who will change their mind about sin and turn to Jesus, trust in His sacrifice, and believe in Him, will be saved and will live forever with Jesus.

(John 3:16; 1 Corinthians 15:1-4)

The apostle Paul said that if anyone offers you any other gospel than the true Gospel, then let them go to their own spiritual death, don't go there with them. (Galatians 1:1-12)

> The Jehovah's Witnesses gospel is false because they teach that Jesus was created by Jehovah. No one can be saved by that gospel. It is a gospel of death. Jesus was not created by Jehovah, Jesus is Jehovah.

The apostle John wrote:

"Whoever believes in the Son has believed the testimony of Jehovah. Whoever does not believe the testimony of Jehovah has made Jehovah a liar because they won't believe the testimony that Jehovah gave of His Son

Whoever has the Son has eternal life; and whoever does not have the Son does not have eternal life. I've written this letter to you who believe in the Son of Jehovah so that you will know that those of you who believe in the Son of Jehovah will live forever."

1 John 5:10-13

Who's the real leader of the Jehovah's Witnesses?
The Jehovah's Witnesses are so dedicated, standing on street corners spreading their message like an army. But the commander in chief of their army is the devil. Their lord and master is the devil.

Who are the devil's decoys?
A decoy is something that people or animals are drawn to because of its attractiveness. But the decoy is fake. It's a trap.

A hunter uses a wooden duck, painted to look like a real duck. The hunter hopes that some poor real duck will <u>think</u> the decoy <u>is</u> a real duck. When the real duck flies to the decoy duck then the hunter shoots the real duck and kills it.

The hunter chops off the real duck's head, strips it of its feathers, roasts the duck, and swallows it up.

The Jehovah's Witnesses are the devil's decoys The devil uses the Jehovah's Witnesses as decoys by painting them up to look like what people <u>think</u> Christians should look like. The devil attracts people to the Jehovah's Witnesses and then strips them of God's Word and swallow them up spiritually. (2 Corinthians 11:13-15; 1 Peter 5:8)

The apostle Paul said that the devil has the power and ability to make himself appear to be a bright, smiling, caring teacher of the one true way, the way of light and life. The devil didn't come to Eve as a disgusting serpent; he came to her disguised as an angel of light.

(Genesis 3:1-7; 2 Corinthians 11:14)

> So, we shouldn't be surprised then that there are people that the devil can use as his agents, his <u>ministers,</u> his decoys. They appear to the <u>untrained</u> eye to be teachers of the one true way of salvation. They use words and ideas that <u>sound</u> correct. But they are bait, a trap meant to trick the unsuspecting and lure them to a spiritual death.

See 2 Corinthians 11:2-4, 13,15; Ephesians 5:6-14; Colossians 2:4-11,18-19; 1 John 4:1-3; 2 John 1:7-11

Can you be saved without the Son of God?

Here's what the apostle John wrote:

"Anyone who believes in the Son of God already has eternal life. But whoever does not believe in the Son of God will not have eternal life because God's anger is on them."   John 3:36

Jesus, the Son of God, said this:

"If a person does not abide in Me, they are cast forth as a branch and they wither. Then people gather them, and cast them into the fire, and they are burned."   - Jesus, John 15:6

So, no, you cannot be saved unless you believe that Jesus is God's own Son, that Jesus is 100% God. The Jehovah's Witnesses are <u>not</u> saved. God's anger is on them because they <u>deceive</u> people by making people <u>think</u> they believe in the Son of God.   (Romans 1:18)

> <u>But it's a lie</u>. They don't believe in the Son. They might teach that Jesus is the "Son of God," but <u>their</u> "Son of God" was <u>created</u> by Jehovah. Their Jesus is zero percent God. The Jehovah's Witnesses Jesus is not the Son of God. He is a <u>fake</u>.   (See Mark 13:5-6)

Chapter six

The Son of man

The Son of man had a secret identity, like Clark Kent did. Jesus was humble and modest, like Clark Kent was. Only a few people knew that Clark Kent was really Superman. And only a few people knew that the Son of man was really the Son of God.   (Matthew 16:13-14)

When Jesus called Himself "the Son of man" He was saying that He was "the Son of humankind." Jesus was both the Son of God and the Son of humankind.

The Son of man is God Himself in a disguise. You don't know who it is. But then He pulls off the disguise and says "Surprise! It's <u>Me</u>, God!"

If a king disguises himself so he can walk unnoticed among the people and find out what they're thinking, he's still the king. God, our King, disguised Himself as one of us and walked among us. But He was still the King.

> If you want to understand who the Son of man is, you can start by doing your own study of two passages. They are Isaiah 53:1-12 and Philippians 2:5-11

The beauty of Heaven is beyond our ability to comprehend. There's nothing that's ugly or evil or offensive. Jesus left that to become one of us. He smelled our toilets and saw our unimaginable acts of evil.

The Son of man felt pain. So much pain that the Bible calls Jesus "a Man of pain" (Isaiah 53:3). Jesus cried. He felt hunger, thirst, tiredness, and holy anger. Jesus felt an unlimited amount of love and compassion, and like us, Jesus experienced death.
(Matthew 15:32; 21:18; 27:26-31;
Mark. 3:5; 4:38; 10:21; John 4:6-7; 11:35-36; 15:9; 19:28,30)

Jesus was exposed to all the earthly temptations that we are. The difference between us and Jesus is that Jesus never gave in to those temptations. Jesus never sinned, meaning He never disobeyed God's laws.   (Matthew 4:1-11; Hebrews 4:15; 1 John 3:4)

Here's what the apostle Paul wrote:

"You know the grace of our Lord Jesus Christ. He was rich, but He
became poor. Jesus did that for us. God became poor, so that through
His poverty, we could become rich."
                                                          2 Corinthians 8:9

> When Jesus came to earth He did not demand all the honor and riches
> that He deserved as our Creator, King, and Judge. Jesus was born into
> a poor family.

How do I know they were poor?
Luke 2:24 says that after she gave birth to Jesus, Mary obeyed the law
of Israel which required her to bring either two turtledove birds or two
young pigeons to the temple as a sacrifice.

If we look at that law, in Leviticus 12:1-8, we see that the required
sacrifice was to be a young lamb and one turtledove or young pigeon.
But if the woman couldn't afford a lamb, then she could bring two
turtledoves or two young pigeons. Joseph and Mary were poor. They
weren't starving, but they weren't wealthy. Are you poor and living in
humble circumstances? Cheer up, so was Jesus.

In addition to putting aside the riches He possessed as God, Jesus also
put aside the dignity which He possessed as God. As a child, Jesus
obeyed His parents, even though Joseph was not His real father, but
only His legal guardian [Luke 2:48,51]. Jesus obeyed the law of Israel
[Galatians 4:4]. Jesus obeyed God [John 10:18]. Jesus became a servant
[Isaiah 49:1-13].
                                   (Mark 6:3; Romans 5:19; Hebrews 2:9-18; 5:8)

> Jesus said:
> "The Son of man did not come to be served, but to serve,
>   and to give His life as a ransom for many sinners."
>   - Jesus, Mark 10:45

Notice what Jesus said. He didn't say, "I came to serve and give My life." Instead, Jesus said, "The Son of man came to serve and give His life." Do you know what that is? It's modesty. Jesus wasn't looking to be honored at an awards ceremony. Jesus did His job in a humble way.

And Jesus taught His followers to do the same:

> "When you have done all the things I order you to do, then call yourselves worthless servants who did your duty."
> - Jesus, Luke 17:10

The apostle Paul followed the example of his Lord and Savior. When talking about how he was taken to Paradise, Paul didn't say, "I was taken." Paul said, "I knew a man who was taken."

(2 Corinthians 12:1-11)

Jesus was humble because people who obey God humble themselves to God:

> "Here's what I, Jehovah, have to say: I look with pleasure at those who are humble, whose hearts have been pierced with sorrow because of their filthiness, and who are dead serious about listening to what I say, and who obey Me."   Isaiah 66:2

Everything except the part about having a heart pierced with sorrow over one's filthiness applies to Jesus. There was no filthiness in Jesus like there is in us.

Why the secret identity?

Jesus couldn't reveal everything right away. He would have been killed sooner. 'The people wanted to kill Jesus because Jesus said He was God's own Son. So Jesus took the humble position and called Himself the Son of man.

Everything had to happen according to God's timing. But as the end neared and the high priest asked Jesus if He was God, Jesus boldly stated that, yes, He is God.   (Matthew 26:62-67)

Before Jesus was in Mary's womb He was <u>not</u> the Son of God or the Son of man. Jesus is the eternal God. Jesus was the Son only from the time He was in Mary's womb, and will be until He delivers up to the Father all those that receive Him as Savior. Then Jesus will return to His eternal position in Heaven.   (Isaiah 9:6; 1 Corinthians 15:24)

The humble Son of man is Jehovah, the King:

"Rejoice greatly, Oh daughter of Zion. Shout, Oh daughter of Jerusalem. Look up, your King will come to you. He is righteous, and He will bring salvation with Him. He will be lowly, and will ride upon a donkey."   Zechariah 9:9

Who is the King? Jehovah is. Who is the Savior? Jehovah. But Zechariah 9:9 is talking about Jesus. How do I know? Because six hundred years after it was written, Jesus was the fulfillment of that prediction in Zechariah 9:9:

"The disciples brought the donkey and put their clothes on it. Then Jesus took His seat on the donkey. A huge crowd spread their clothing on the path that Jesus was to take. And some cut down branches from the trees and scattered them along the way.

People walked in front of and behind Jesus. They were shouting, 'Hosanna to the Son of David! Blessed is He who comes in the name of Jehovah. Hosanna in the highest!'

And when Jesus arrived in Jerusalem, all the people were stirred up. They were asking, 'Who <u>is</u> this?'

And the crowds that were with Jesus said, 'This is Jesus the Prophet from Nazareth in Galilee.'"   Matthew 21:7-11

That's Jehovah, God Himself, our Creator, riding into Jerusalem, as King, on a donkey. What does "Hosanna" mean? It means "Save us now." God became the Son of man to save us from our sins.

Who called Jesus the Son of man?

In the <u>four Gospels</u> the <u>only one</u> who called Jesus the Son of man was Jesus Himself. It was the name Jesus used most for Himself. Jesus called Himself the Son of man dozens of times.

The <u>first time</u> Jesus was called the Son of man is when Jesus Himself said this:

"The Son of man has no home to lay down His head."
- Jesus, Matthew 8:20

And the <u>last time</u> Jesus was called the Son of man was when this was said about Him:

"And I, John, looked, and I saw a white cloud, and sitting on the cloud was One who looked exactly like the Son of man. He had a gold crown on His head, and a sharp sickle in His hand."
Revelation 14:14

Jesus, the Son of man, humbled Himself to become a homeless man. But because He obeyed His Father in Heaven, then God elevated Jesus to the highest position. Jesus will return as the Judge. Jesus went from humiliation to glorification.   (Psalms 2:6-9; 110:1-2; Ezekiel 21:27; Matthew 28:18; Acts 1:11; 2:32-33; Revelation 19:11-16)

The death of the Son of man was predicted in Daniel 9:24-26, and His return as the Judge, was predicted in Daniel 7:13-14.

Jesus said this:

"When the Son of man returns in His glory, with all the holy angels, then He will sit upon the throne of His glory. And people from every nation will be brought to face Him. And He will separate them like a shepherd separates the sheep from the goats.

He will put the sheep at His right hand, but the goats at His left. Then the King will say to them at His right hand, 'Come, ye blessed of My Father, inherit the kingdom prepared for you from the foundation of the world.'"

- Jesus, the King and the Judge, Matthew 25:31-34

The Jehovah's Witnesses are going to throw some hard questions at you to try and confuse you. They will ask you why Jesus said things like,

- "I say the things that I heard from My Father; I do not say or do anything from Myself; but as My Father taught Me, I speak these things."   John 8:26,28

- "But as far as when the day and hour will be, no one knows. Not even the angels in Heaven. Not even the Son. Only the Father knows." Mark 13:32

- "My Father is greater than Me."   John 14:28

And why does 1 Corinthians 15:28 say that the Son will be subject to the Father?

> Someone who wants to confuse you will only show you one side and try to make you think it's the only side. We're taught to study the Bible diligently, to search through the Bible, and to rightly divide, which means you put things where they belong. Look to our Guide.
> (Acts 17:11; 2 Timothy 2:15; Hebrews 11:6)

All the verses I just showed you on this page are talking about the Son of man, the secret identity of Jesus, the humble Jesus, Jesus the man. When the Jehovah's Witnesses ask you about a verse, tell them you'll write it down. Then go and read commentaries on that verse and do your own study. Ask God for wisdom.   (James 1:5-8)

When Superman appeared, people would say, "Look, up in the sky ... it's a bird ... it's a plane — it's Superman!" And one day Jesus will appear in the sky. Everyone will see Him. Everyone will see His secret identity. And everyone will fall to their knees before Him. Those who love Him will fall with obedient love and respect. But His enemies will fall in fear, stiff as boards.   (Matthew 24:44;
1 Corinthians 16:22; 2 Thessalonians 3:5;
2 Timothy 4:8; 1 Peter 1:7; Revelation 1:7; 6:15-17)

Chapter seven

How are Jesus and Jehovah one?

"Jehovah and Me are one"

- Jesus, John 10:30

The word <u>one</u> means <u>one</u> — <u>not</u> <u>two</u>. If God created Jesus, and Jesus is the archangel Michael, as the Jehovah's Witnesses teach, then that would make <u>two</u>.

But Jesus <u>did</u> <u>not</u> say, "Jehovah and Me are <u>two</u>." Jesus said, "Jehovah and Me are <u>one</u>."

When Jesus was dying on the cross, He loudly cried out:

"Father, I put My soul in Your hands."   Luke 23:46

> Jesus breathed His last breath right after He said those words. Jesus died on the cross.

Now, look at this:
The evil men who killed Jesus found two witnesses who would testify falsely against Jesus at His unlawful trial.   (Matthew 26:59-61)

And the same thing happened to a disciple of Jesus, named Stephen. Evil men wanted to kill Stephen, so they found men who would testify falsely against him.   (Acts 6:8-11)

They violently grabbed Stephen, dragged him to their unlawful trial, and made him stand in front of them. As they stared at Stephen they saw that Stephen's face looked like the face of an angel.
    (Acts 6:12-15)

Those evil men were filled with anger, and they gnashed on Stephen with their teeth. But Stephen was filled with the Holy Spirit.

And it was as though Stephen didn't notice what they were doing to him. He was staring up at the sky as though he was watching something. Stephen saw the glory of God, and Jesus, standing at the right hand of God.   (Acts 7:54-55)

Then Stephen said,

"Look! I see the sky opening up, and the Son of man standing at the right hand of God."   Acts 7:56

When the evil men heard Stephen say that, they put their hands over their ears. They hated it. It drove them mad. They all ran at Stephen, dragged him out of the city, and threw stones at him.   (Acts 7:57-58)

Stephen cried out, saying,

> "Lord Jesus, receive my soul."   Acts 7:59

Then Stephen knelt down, and cried out loudly, "Lord, do not charge them with this sin."

And after he said that, Stephen died.

(Acts 7:60; See Luke 23:34)

• Now, what did Jesus say just before He died on the cross? He said, "Father, I put My soul in Your hands."   (Luke 23:46)

• But just before Stephen died, what did he say? Stephen said, "Lord Jesus, receive my soul."   (Acts 7:59)

Why did Stephen ask Jesus to receive his soul? Why didn't Stephen put his soul in God's hands like Jesus did? Because Jesus is God. If you ask Jesus to receive your soul it's the same thing as putting your soul in God's hands.

Would Stephen put his soul in Michael's hands? Never! Don't believe the evil lie that Jesus is Michael. If Michael heard the Jehovah's Witnesses say that, he would tell them to shut up.

Who is the Shepherd?

The **Old Testament** says this:

"Listen to this! Jehovah the Lord will come with His mighty strength, and rule with His arm. Hear this! He will bring rewards with Him. It's payday! Jehovah will feed His flock like a shepherd. He will pick up the lambs into His arms, and carry them next to His heart. And He will gently lead those that are with young ones."   Isaiah 40:10-11

In the **New Testament**, Jesus said:

"I am the good Shepherd, and I know My sheep"   John 10:14

After Jesus resurrected from the dead, and just before He returned to Heaven, He confronted the apostle Peter. Jesus asked Peter three times, "Do you love Me? And three times Peter said, "Yes, Lord, I love you." And Jesus responded by saying, "Feed My lambs," "Feed My sheep," "Feed My sheep."   (John 21:15-17)

Jesus said, "I am the Shepherd," and Jesus called the believers, "My lambs, My sheep." But we just read in Isaiah that the sheep and the lambs belong to Jehovah, and that Jehovah is the Shepherd.

Everyone knows the first line of the 23rd Psalm:

"The Lord is my Shepherd, I shall not want." Psalms 23:1 (KJV)

In the original Hebrew, the words, "The Lord" is "Jehovah." So, it really says, "Jehovah is my Shepherd."

What does the **New Testament** say?

"The God of peace raised our Lord Jesus, the great Shepherd of the sheep, from death, through the blood of the everlasting covenant."
                                     Hebrews 13:20

Jesus is Jehovah, the great Shepherd.

Jehovah forgives sins:

• "I, even I, am Jehovah, the One who blots out your rebellions for My own sake. And I will not remember your sins."   Isaiah 43:25

• "I, Jehovah, will erase their guilt, and I will remember their sin no more."   Jeremiah 31:34

• "I am Jehovah, Jehovah God. I am merciful and gracious, and I bear with My people. I give them an abundance of goodness and faithfulness.

"I show mercy to all who love Me by taking away their perverseness and rebellion and sin."   Exodus 34:6-7

Jesus forgives sins:

A wonderful thing happened one time when Jesus visited the town of Capernaum. People saw where Jesus went, and they were telling everybody, "Jesus is in the house!" So everybody poured into the house. They were packed like sardines. And Jesus taught them the Word of God.

Then, four people came to the house. They were carrying a paralyzed man on a mattress. They wanted to see Jesus. But it was impossible. Too many people. So they carried the man up to the roof and they made a hole in the roof. You could do that with the kind of roofs they had. Then they lowered the man on his mattress, through the hole in the roof.   (Mark 2:1-4)

> When Jesus saw how much faith they had in Him, He said to the paralyzed man, "Son, your sins are forgiven."   (Mark 2:5)

But there were some religious authorities in the crowd
Those so-called religious authorities heard Jesus tell the man that his sins were forgiven. They were thinking — Why is this man doing such an evil thing, forgiving a person's sins? Only God can forgive sins!
(Mark 2:7)

Jesus knew what the men were thinking because Jesus is God. Jesus asked them why they had those feelings in their hearts. Jesus asked them, "Which would be easier to say to the paralyzed man: 'You're sins are forgiven' or to say, 'Stand up, pick up your mattress, and go home and live your life?'"

And as soon as Jesus said that, the paralyzed man stood up, picked up his mattress, and went home, while everyone watched. The people were amazed. They glorified God, and said, "We've never seen anything like that before." (Mark 2:8-12)

When Jesus said to that man, "Son, your sins are forgiven," in front of all those people, Jesus was boldly, clearly, emphatically telling us that He is God.

When the men were thinking, "Why is this man doing evil by forgiving sins? Only God can forgive sins!" Jesus didn't say, "Oh, sorry, you misunderstood. I'm not God" No, Jesus dug in deeper.

When Jesus forgave the man of his sins, Jesus was saying, "I am Jehovah, God."

See the account in Luke 7:36-46, which leads up to the especially important words spoken by Jesus to a Pharisee and to a humble woman in Luke 7:47-50. Only God Himself could say what Jesus said to them.

In the Old Testament, **Jehovah** said this:

"I am Jehovah, and there is no other God besides Me. I am the righteous God, and the Savior. There is none besides Me.

Look to Me, and you will be saved, whoever you are and wherever you are. I am God, and no one else is.

I have sworn by Myself, the Word has gone out of My mouth in righteousness, and it will never change.

And I say that everyone will <u>fall down on their knees</u> to Me, and everyone will admit that I am Jehovah."

- Jehovah, Isaiah 45:21-23

The New Testament tells us what will happen when **Jesus** returns:

"Everyone will <u>fall down on their knees</u> to Jesus.

Everyone, including those who are in Heaven, and those who are living on earth, and the wicked who have died and are awaiting judgment.

And everyone will admit that Jesus is Jehovah."

Philippians 2:10-11

The Hebrew language of the Old Testament would sometimes get people's attention by repeating something twice, and even three times. And many Hebrew forms of expression like that were used in the New Testament.

Here are some examples: In Isaiah 26:3 the words "perfect peace" are "peace, peace" in the original Hebrew; Jeremiah 7:4: "the temple of Jehovah, the temple of Jehovah, the temple of Jehovah;" John 13:20: "Verily, verily;" and Revelation 4:8: "Holy, holy, holy."

I bring this up because of what I'm going to show you now.

Three times in the Old Testament, **Jehovah** said this:

 • "Who is it who has created and accomplished, forming all the people of the world from the beginning? I have, Jehovah, <u>the first with the last</u>. I am."   Isaiah 41:4

 • "Here's what I Jehovah say: I am the King of Israel, and Israel's Kinsman Redeemer, the Lord of Heaven's armies. <u>I am the first and I am the last</u>. And besides Me there is no God."   Isaiah 44:6

 • "Obey Me, Oh Jacob and Israel, those that I have called to Me. I am He. <u>I, Jehovah, am the first, I also am the last</u>."   Isaiah 48:12

Three times in the New Testament, **Jesus** said this:

 • "Don't be afraid, <u>I am the first and the last</u>."   Revelation 1:17

 • "<u>The first and the last</u> is saying these things."   Revelation 2:8

 • "I am Alpha and Omega, the Beginning and the End,
    <u>the First and the Last</u>."   Revelation 22:13

Only Jehovah and Jesus said "I am the first and the last" because only Jehovah and Jesus <u>can</u> say that. Jesus is Jehovah.

One day, the people said to Jesus, "How long will You keep us in suspense? Do You claim to be the Christ? Just tell us!" John 10:24

And Jesus said, "I already told you that I'm the Christ, and you didn't believe Me because you're not My sheep. My sheep know My voice, and I know them. My sheep follow Me and I give them eternal life, and they will never die" John 10:25-28

Then Jesus did something very interesting. First, Jesus said:

- "No one can take My sheep out of My hand." John 10:28

Then Jesus said,

- "No one can take My sheep out of Jehovah's hand." John 10:29

Then, Jesus followed that up by saying:

- "Me and Jehovah are one." John 10:30

Now, I know that certain people will make their dumb argument that when Jesus said that He and Jehovah are one that He just meant they both had the same interests. Oh, please.

The people sure knew He didn't mean that. They picked up stones to kill Jesus. They said, "We're going to kill You because you're a man, and You're making Yourself God!" John 10:31-33 (See Leviticus 24:16)

Did Jesus apologize? Did He tell them they misunderstood? No! That means they were right when they said He claimed to be God.

Jesus said that believers are held in His hand. And Jesus said that believers are held in Jehovah's hand. A created being can't say that. Michael the archangel can't say that, nor would he dare. Only God can hold believers in His hand. Jesus is once again telling us that He and Jehovah are one, one and the same.

Jehovah called Himself the Holy One:

"I am God, and not a man. <u>I am the Holy One</u>."
- Jehovah, Hosea 11:9
(See Isaiah 29:23; 43:3; 49:7)

King David called **Jehovah** the Holy One:

"I will praise You while I play a stringed musical instrument because <u>You are True</u> and Faithful. It's to You that I will sing while I play, because You are the Holy One of Israel."   Psalms 71:22

<u>And</u> king David called **Jesus** the Holy One:

"You, Jehovah, will not leave me in the place where the dead go. You will not let Your Holy One's body decay."   Psalms 16:10

David said, "me," but David is talking about Jesus. And when David says, "the Holy One," he's talking about Jesus. I can prove it.

Here's what the **apostle Peter** said:

"People of Israel, listen to what I have to say. God proved to you that the Man, Jesus of Nazareth, was sent by Him. How did God prove it? All of you saw the power that Jesus had. He did all kinds of miraculous, impossible things. That was it, that was the sign, the proof that God sent Jesus.

God planned all along to turn Jesus over to you. He knew that your wicked hands would nail Jesus to a cross. But God raised Jesus from the dead, and freed Him from the sorrows of death, so that He would not be held by it, as king David predicted."   Acts 2:22-24

Then Peter went on and quoted the words we just read, the words David wrote in Psalms 16:10 about "not leaving my soul in the place where the dead go." That proves that David was talking about Jesus.

Jehovah called Himself the Holy One. David called Jehovah the Holy One. David and Peter called Jesus the Holy One.

And **Jesus** called Himself the Holy One:

"To the believers of the church in Philadelphia: I who say these things is He who is the Holy One, He who is True, He who has the key of David, He who opens, and no one shuts, and shuts, and no one opens." - Jesus, Revelation 3:7

Does your Bible say, "He who is Holy," instead of "He who is the Holy One"? It's the same thing. This is talking about total holiness. Only God can refer to Himself as "He who is Holy" or "He who is the Holy One."

Who else knew that **Jesus** is the Holy One?

The angel **Gabriel** said this to Mary:

"The Holy Spirit will come to you, and the power of the Most High will rest upon you. That's why the Holy One who will be born through you will be called God's Son." Luke 1:35

An **evil spirit** knew that **Jesus** is the Holy One:

"There was a man who was possessed by an unclean, evil spirit. When Jesus approached the man, the evil spirit cried out in a loud voice, saying, 'Leave us alone; what have we to do with You, Jesus of Nazareth? Have You come to destroy us? I know who You are. You are the Holy One of God.'

Then Jesus put the evil spirit out of business by saying to him, 'I order your jaws to shut tight. Now get away from that man.' Then, when the evil spirit convulsed, the man was thrown into the midst of the people, unhurt. And astonishment came upon all the people, and they said, 'What a Word He speaks!'" Luke 4:33-36

The Jehovah's Witnesses do not know that Jesus is the Holy One

Jesus gives the breath of life:

"Jesus said to His disciples, 'Peace to you. My Father sent Me, and now I'm sending you.'

And after Jesus said that, He breathed on the disciples, and said to them, 'Receive a first taste of the Holy Spirit's power from on high.'"
- Jesus, John 20:21-22

Jehovah gives the breath of life:

Jehovah told Ezekiel to talk to dry bones, and say:

"Oh you dry bones, hear the Word of the Lord. Jehovah said 'I will breathe into you, and you will live. I will restore your flesh and skin, and I will put My breath in you so that you will live, and you will know that I am Jehovah, your Lord.'"
Ezekiel 37:4-6

Jehovah showed the prophet Ezekiel a valley full of very dry bones. Those bones represented the people. The people were dry spiritually because they weren't getting the living water from the Word of God. They were being led by false shepherds who gave them lies instead of truth.

The breath that came from the mouth of Jesus and gave the disciples a first taste of the Holy Spirit's life-giving power is the <u>same</u> breath that Jehovah breathed into those dry bones.

The breath of Jesus is the same breath that gave life to Adam in Genesis 2:7. It is God's breath, the breath of life. God's Holy Spirit gives life, eternal life.

Jehovah made it clear that He is the only Savior:

"I am Jehovah. Yes, Me, Jehovah. And there is no savior besides
Me."   - Jehovah, Isaiah 43:11

But what about this?

"From Simon Peter, a servant and an apostle of Jesus Christ, to those
who have been given the same precious faith through the
righteousness of God and our Savior Jesus Christ."
                                          2 Peter 1:1

If God said there is no Savior besides Him and the Bible calls Jesus the
Savior, then what does that mean? Two Saviors? Never.

God told us the answer:

"Listen to what I, Jehovah, am saying to you. The day will come
when I will raise up a Son of David. He will be a righteous Branch, and
a King. He will use wisdom to be the enforcer. He will use integrity to
make real justice in the land.

That's when Judah will be saved, and Israel will live in peace and
security.

And here's the name that this righteous Branch will be called:
JEHOVAH OUR RIGHTEOUSNESS."

                                          - Jehovah, Jeremiah 23:5-6

That's Jehovah speaking there. He's talking about the one who will
save. The one He calls the righteous Branch, the Son of David. He's
talking about Jesus. And Jehovah said that Jesus will be called
JEHOVAH OUR RIGHTEOUSNESS.

The answer is that Jesus is Jehovah. Jesus is the one speaking in Isaiah
43:11; Jesus said, "I am Jehovah, and there is no savior besides Me."
The name Jesus means, "Jehovah our Savior." Jesus is the only Savior.

"The Samaritans said to the woman, 'We're no longer just going by what you told us about Jesus. Now we've heard Jesus speak. And now <u>we</u> know that Jesus truly is the Savior of the world.'"
John 4:42

Were they wrong?

Now someone might tell you that the Samaritans were mistaken, that they just thought Jesus was the Savior.

No. After the Samaritans said that, Jesus did not tell them to stop speaking evil words. Jesus didn't tell them that only Jehovah is the Savior and therefore He can't be the Savior. No, Jesus let them believe that He is the Savior. Why? Because Jesus <u>is</u> <u>the</u> Savior! Jesus stayed with the Samaritans for two days after they said that He was the Savior of the world. (John 4:43)

Jehovah is Jesus the Savior

"Our Savior's name is Jehovah, Israel's Holy One, the Lord of Heaven's armies." Isaiah 47:4

Jesus said this to Martha:

"I am Resurrection and I am Eternal Life. Yes, people's bodies made of flesh and blood and bones, will die. But even though their body dies, every one of them who believes in Me will live, and I mean they will live with Me — forever."
- Jesus, John 11:25

The Old Testament says this about **Jehovah**:

> "Jehovah, your God, He is God of gods and Lord of lords."
> Deuteronomy 10:17

> "Oh give thanks to Jehovah, He truly is good, and His loving kindness is forever.
>
> Oh give thanks to the God of gods, His love is forever.
>
> Oh give thanks to the Lord of lords, His mercy is forever."
> Psalms 136:1-3

The New Testament says this about **Jesus**:

> "The ten kings will engage in warfare with the Lamb, and the Lamb will overcome them because He is Lord of lords and King of kings. And they that fight with the Lamb are those who are called, and chosen, and faithful." Revelation 17:14

Jesus is the Lamb: (Isaiah 53:7-8; John 1:29,35-36; Acts 8:32; 1 Peter 1:18-20; Revelation 1:18; 5:6-14; 12:10-11; 19:5-9)

When Jesus returns to judge and make war, He will be wearing this name:

King of kings and Lord of lords

See Revelation 19:11-21

Who are believers baptized into?

In Matthew 28:19 Jesus told the apostles to baptize people into the name of the Father, and of the Son, and of the Holy Spirit.

The Jehovah's Witnesses tell people that Jesus is a created being and that the Holy Spirit is not a person. If that were true, then why in the world would Jehovah include <u>them</u> in the believer's baptism?

> If only Jehovah was God then Jesus would have told the apostles to only baptize people in the name of the Father, Jehovah. But Jesus is God. And the Holy Spirit <u>is</u> a person. The Holy Spirit is God.

Later, in Acts 2:38, the apostle Peter told people to be baptized into the name of Jesus Christ.

Peter names Jesus without mentioning the Father or the Holy Spirit. Why is that? Because when you have Jesus you have the Father and the Holy Spirit. Everything there is to God is in Jesus.

(See Colossians 2:9)

The Old Testament says this about **Jehovah**:

> "Jehovah is in His holy temple, Jehovah's throne is in Heaven.
>
> His eyes carefully consider, His eyelids examine, and He determines the condition of every person.
>
> Jehovah refines the righteous person, like gold:
> but He hates the wicked person, and He hates the person who loves to be cruel."
>
> Psalms 11:4-5

In the New Testament, **Jesus** said this:

> "Yes, you're doing good things, you church in Thyatira. But I have something against you. You allow the woman Jezebel, who calls herself a prophetess, to seduce My servants into engaging in the most evil practices of the idol worshipers, and to eat things that have been sacrificed to idols.
>
> And I gave her time, hoping that she would repent, but she refused to repent of her idol worship. Hear this! I'm throwing her and all those who commit adultery with her into a bed of great anguish. If they don't change their mind, then I will kill her disciples with death.
>
> And all the churches will know that I am the One who examines people's innermost thoughts, feelings, and desires. And I will give to each of you what you deserve, based on what you do."
>
> Revelation 2:20-23

Both Jehovah and Jesus know what's in the hearts of every one of us, our innermost thoughts and desires. No created being can do that. Michael can't do that. Only God can.

The Old Testament says this:

> "A Child will be born to a woman who had never touched a man.
> And she will give that Child the name Emmanuel." Isaiah 7:14

That Child was born 600 years later. Matthew 1:21-25 tells us that the woman, Mary, gave birth to a Son, even though she had never been with a man. She named Him Jesus because He would save His people from their sins. The name Jesus means, "Jehovah, our Savior."

And we're told that the birth of Mary's Child <u>was the fulfillment</u> of the prediction in Isaiah 7:14, that a woman, a virgin, would have a Son, and that the Son would be called Emmanuel. What does Emmanuel mean? Matthew 1:23 tells us that Emmanuel means "God with us."

In Revelation, chapter 21, the apostle John was allowed to see a vision of what will happen at the beginning of the eternity to come. Here's what John said:

> "I, John, saw the holy city, new Jerusalem, coming down from God out of Heaven, dazzling, like a bride all decked out for her husband.
>
> And I heard a great voice out of Heaven saying, 'Look up! God's home has come down to the people. And God will live with them, and they will be His people.
>
> And God Himself will be with them, and be <u>God with us</u>.
>
> And God will wipe away all the tears from their eyes. There will be no more death, no more sadness or crying. There will never be any more pain. All those things will pass away.'"

> Revelation 21:2-4

That's talking about Jehovah. God with us is Jehovah.

> Who is God with us? Jesus is. Jesus is God with us and Jehovah is God with us.

Two Gods? Never. A God and a god? No way. Jehovah and Michael? No! There is only one God. His name is Jehovah and His name is Jesus. He is the one who loves us, who gave Himself for us. He is the one who will wipe away our tears. Not Michael.

In Isaiah 8:8, Jehovah is called, "Oh Emmanuel."

Isaiah 8:10 says this to the enemies of Israel:

"Go ahead, get together and make your plans. They will amount to nothing. Go ahead, give your army the shout to attack us. It will not stand. Why? Because God is with us."

Isaiah 8:10

In that verse, Isaiah 8:10, what is "God is with us" in the original Hebrew? It is "Emmanuel." Who is Emmanuel? The Book of Isaiah says that Jehovah is Emmanuel. And the Gospel of Matthew says that Jesus is Emmanuel.

Who can calm the sea?

The Old Testament says this:

> "Those who go down to the sea in ships,
>   who work in great waters;
>
> They are the ones who see the wonderful things
>   that Jehovah does in the deep sea.
>
> Their ships lift up to the sky and come down to the depths
>   when Jehovah commands the stormy wind
>   that lifts up the waves.
>
> Their hearts melt with fear because of the danger.
> They are thrown this way and that way, like a drunken person.
> And it's as though all their knowledge of the sea and sailing
>   skills have been swallowed up by the waves.
>
> Then they cry to Jehovah in their anguish
>   and Jehovah calms their fear by calming the storm
>   so that the waves become quiet.
>
> Then they are glad because of what Jehovah did, as
>   Jehovah gently guides them to their favorite safe place.
>
> All of us should thank Jehovah for His goodness
>   and all the wonderful things He does for us."
>
>   Psalms 107:23-31

But what about those who die at sea?

That's right. The seas don't always become calm and many die at sea. But this Bible passage is comparing people who work in a ship in the deep sea to what life is like for those who work for God. We live in a world where there is much evil. Believers have times of danger because of it. God lets it happen to us. But here God is reminding believers that our <u>souls</u> are held safely in His hands. And even if we are killed in the line of duty, He will bring us safely to Heaven to be with Him forever.

"When it was evening, Jesus said to the apostles,
 'Let's sail over to the other side of the sea.'
 So the apostles took Jesus with them in the boat.

But there arose a big storm, with strong winds.
 The waves were coming into the boat
 and the boat was filling with water.
 While this was going on, Jesus was sound asleep
 at the other end of the boat, with His head on a cushion.

The apostles woke Jesus up and said to Him:
 'Teacher, don't You care that we are dying?'
 When Jesus was fully awake He told the wind to back off.
 Jesus said to the sea, 'Stand still, be quiet.'
 Then the wind stopped, and there was absolute calm.

Jesus said to the apostles, 'Why are you so fearful?
 Why don't you have any faith?'

But now the apostles really wanted to get out of that boat.
 When they saw what Jesus did it scared them half to death.
 They were terrified.

They said to each other, 'Who is this Man?
 He can even make the wind and the sea obey Him.'"
 Mark 4:35-41

The apostles weren't afraid of the wind and sea anymore. Now they were terrified because they realized they were sitting in a boat with God Himself. They were in the presence of the One who can make the sea and wind obey Him. They knew that only Jehovah could do that. No one needed to tell them who Jesus was now.

Now they knew that they were sitting in a boat with their Creator, the eternal God, their loving God, their Judge, Jehovah Himself.

Jehovah created everything:

"Here's what I, Jehovah, your Savior, have to say. I'm the one who assembled your bodies in your mother's wombs. It was My idea! That's right. And listen to <u>this</u>: Every single thing that exists — I did that!

That sky that you look up at — I stretched that all out. And that planet, earth, that you walk around on – I hammered that out. And do you know who helped Me? Nobody! I did it all by Myself. Me, Jehovah, and no one else."   - Jehovah, Isaiah 44:24

The Jehovah's Witnesses teach that Jehovah was all alone, and that then Jehovah created Jesus, and then Jesus created everything else: our bodies, our planet, the universe, and everything in it. But here, in Isaiah 44:24, Jehovah is saying that those so-called Jehovah's Witnesses are not telling you the truth.

(See Isaiah 45:18; Revelation 4:10-11)

Jesus created everything:

"Everything that was created was created by Jesus. And there is not even one single thing that was created by anyone other than Jesus."
John 1:3

"Everything that was created was created by Jesus. Everything in the sky and everything on the earth; everything in the physical world and everything in the spirit world, from the highest to the lowest, from the greatest to the least.

Everything that exists was created by Jesus and for Jesus. Before anything was created, Jesus already was. And Jesus holds together everything that He created."
Colossians 1:16-17

Jesus is Jehovah the Creator.

Who is the light of the world?

In the Old Testament, **Jehovah** said this:

"You won't need the sun anymore to give you light during the day, and you won't have the moon shining at night. That's because I, Jehovah, will give you light. I will be your beautiful light, forever and ever."   - Jehovah, Isaiah 60:19

In the New Testament, **Jesus** said this:

"I am the light of the world."   - Jesus, John 8:12

Michael the archangel would never say "I am the light of the world." No created being would dare say such a thing, except maybe the devil.

When Jesus said, "I am the light of the world," Jesus could not have said it more simply or more boldly or more clearly that He is God.

See Malachi 4:1-3. There is only one who brings the brightness of God. He is the Light, the <u>Sun</u> of righteousness. There is only one Healer, and that is the one Lord and Savior, Jesus Christ.

(See Psalms 97:11; John 1:4-9; 3:19;
Acts 26:18; Ephesians 5:13-14;
1Thessalonians 5:5; 1 John 1:7; Revelation 21:23)

Chapter eight

Only Jesus

Jesus made a whip. He used that whip to drive out everybody who was in the temple making it a place of business. Jesus drove out the sheep and the oxen that they were selling. He poured out the money from their cash registers onto the floor, and overturned their tables. Jesus called the temple, "My Father's house."   (John 2:13-17)

The people saw this as something that could only be done by the Messiah who was predicted in the Old Testament, the King and Savior, who would be God Himself. So they asked Jesus to give them a sign to prove to them that He had the authority to clear out the temple like He did.   (John 2:18)

Jesus just gave them a sign!
That <u>was</u> the sign, the way Jesus cleared the temple and called the temple, "My Father's house."   (Malachi 3:1-3)

Jesus answered their question though. He said, "Destroy this Temple, and in three days I will raise it up." The people said, "It took forty-six years to build the Temple. Will You rebuild it in three days? But Jesus spoke of "the Temple of His body."   (John 2:19-21)

They didn't understand that Jesus was predicting His death, and claiming that three days after He dies He will raise Himself from death and return to life in His very same flesh body.

No created being has that kind of power over their life. No created being can say they will lay down their life and then take back their life again. Only God Himself could say He would do that and then actually do it. Only Jesus could do that.

Jesus said:

"No one takes My life from Me. I lay it down Myself. I have the power to lay it down, and I have the power to take it again. I have been ordered to do this by My Father."   - Jesus, John 10:18

What did Jesus do for a humble woman?

Jesus was at the house of a man named Simon, in a town called
Bethany. A woman came to the house. She was carrying a box made of
valuable stone, like marble. The box contained a precious substance
made from the highest quality oils and perfumes.

And while Jesus was sitting and eating with the others, the woman
broke open the box and poured the oil on His head.   (Matthew 26:6-7)

Matthew writes that the disciples of Jesus were annoyed when they
saw what the woman did. They said to her, "What a waste! We could
have sold that oil for a lot of money that could have been given to the
poor."   (Matthew 26:8)

When Jesus heard that, He said this to His disciples:

"Why are you beating up on this woman? She has done a good work
for Me. Either way you'll always have poor people with you. But you
won't always have Me with you.

There's a reason why she poured that on My body. She did it for
My burial.

And truly I say to you, that everywhere the Gospel will ever be
preached, in the whole world, what this woman has just done for Me
will also be told in remembrance of her."
                                          - Jesus, Matthew 26:10-13

Only God Himself could say that would happen and then see to it that
it did happen. Only God has that power. And notice that Jesus said
"Truly I say to you..." Jesus spoke with an authority that is only
possessed by God Himself.

Here we are, two thousand years after Jesus said that and we can
picture that scene, see that woman, hear the ignorance of the disciples.
We feel the love the woman felt for Jesus. And we are astonished that
she understood that Jesus was her Savior who would die for her,
something the disciples of Jesus didn't know.

And we can so relate to the way Jesus defended that woman. And Jesus did more than defend her against the rude accusation of His disciples. He made sure that everyone, everywhere, forever, knew what she did.

That was God Himself speaking!

Do you understand now that it was God Himself who said that, and did that for her, for that humble woman? Do you feel a warmth in your chest and wetness in your eyes? Is your heart melting? Is the Holy Spirit working on you?

Jesus said:

"They will see the Son of man arriving, leading His army, with great power and glory. And then He will send out His angels, and He will gather His people together, from the ends of the earth and the heavens."   - Jesus, Mark 13:26-27

Look at the power that Jesus is claiming for Himself. That's God's power, God's role. And look, Jesus will send His angels. Jesus isn't an angel. Jesus created the angels, they work for Jesus, only Jesus.

Who will put the devil out of business?

Jesus said:

"How can someone enter the strong man's house and strip him of his weapons unless he first ties up the strong man? Then he will strip the strong man's house."   - Jesus, Matthew 12:29

The strong man in this story is the devil. And the one who will tie up the devil and strip him of his weapons is the Lord Jesus Christ, only Jesus.

Who will crush the devil's head?

Genesis 3:15 tells us what will happen in the distant future. The devil will have Jesus unjustly killed on a cross. The devil is under a death sentence because of that. The devil will never repent. He's a dead man walking. Jesus will carry out the death sentence on the devil. The devil will go to hell and be turned to ashes. Only Jesus gets to do that because Jesus is God the Judge.   (Isaiah 14:15; Ezekiel 28:18; Luke 22:3)

Jesus will ride in on a white horse. His clothing will be stained with blood. Jesus will have a sword, and the name King of kings and Lord of lords. Jesus will kill His enemies with that sword. And Jesus will crush the devil's head.   (Revelation 19:11-21; 20:10)

No, you don't. Unless you know Jesus, because Jesus is the only one who was born into this world without having a human father. Jesus was called the Son of God to teach us that Jesus had a relationship with God that no one else has.

The prophet Isaiah wrote this:

   "The Lord Himself will give you this sign: Listen to this carefully! A virgin will conceive and bear a Son, and she will call His name, Emmanuel."   Isaiah 7:14

That was a prediction of the birth of Jesus. It was written down by the prophet Isaiah under the direction of God's Holy Spirit. It was written around 600 years before Jesus was born. How do I know it's a prediction of the birth of Jesus? I'll tell you.

What does the word **conceive** mean?
God sent the angel Gabriel to a woman named Mary and told her that starting immediately she will have the very beginning of a human life growing inside her body, in her womb. That's what's meant by conceive. Gabriel told Mary that when the Child inside her is born, she is to call His name Jesus. And Jesus will be called the Son of the Most High (God).   (Luke 1:26-32)

What does the word **virgin** mean?
We learn the meaning of the word virgin in the response that Mary gave to the angel Gabriel. Mary said:

"I've never had sex, so how will this Child come to be in my womb?"   Luke 1:34

Gabriel told Mary that this Child will not have a human father. This will be something that's never happened before. It's something that only God can do. This Child will not be the result of a sexual act. Instead, this Child will be placed in her womb when God covers her in the gentle power of His creative ability, through His Holy Spirit.

Only Jesus was born that way, no one else. Only Jesus can say that God is His own Father. And that's why the Holy One that Mary gave birth to is called God's Son. (Luke 1:35)

Why was Jesus born to a virgin? It was a sign. It was done to show us that this One is God. Only God could be born to a virgin. Mary got pregnant without having sex. She had no contact in any way with a man that could have made her pregnant.

Mary is the only woman who was still a virgin after she gave birth. It means Jesus is God. God's not going to do that for an angel, or for any created being.

The fact that Jesus was conceived in a woman's womb, not by a man, but by the power of God's Holy Spirit, proves that Jesus is God

And yes, Matthew 1:22-23 says that Jesus is the Child whose birth was predicted in Isaiah 7:14, whose name is Emmanuel, which means, "God with us."

Who spoke with the same authority as God?

Jesus sat on the side of a mountain and spoke what's known as the Sermon on the Mount.   (Matthew 5:1 to 7:27)

When Jesus finished, the people were astonished by His teachings. They said that Jesus did not teach them like their usual teachers, called "scribes." They said that when Jesus taught them it was as though His mouth was God's mouth.   (Matthew 7:28-29)

In the Old Testament, when the prophets spoke for God, they always said, "This is what the Lord says."

Here are a few of the many times they said that: Jeremiah 7:3; Amos 7:17; Obadiah 1:1; Nahum 1:12; Haggai 2:23; Zechariah 1:3; Malachi 1:4

Jesus spoke like only God can speak
Jesus never said, "This is what the Lord says." Jesus said, "Verily, verily, I say to you." Jesus spoke with the same authority as God because Jesus is God.

The expression Verily, verily means Truly, truly, or Amen, amen. Jesus called Himself, "the Amen" in Revelation 3:14. In Isaiah 65:16 Jehovah is called the "God of amen." The King James Version says, "God of truth." But the original Hebrew for "truth" in this verse is amen, # 543.

I did a quick count and it looks like Jesus started a statement by saying, "Verily, verily" around 70 times. You can see that by looking up the word "verily" in your Strong's Concordance.

> During the Sermon on the Mount Jesus used another expression that no human teacher would dare use.

Jesus said, "But I say to you," as in,

"You've heard how people have added to God's commandment (in Leviticus 19:18). God said you are to love your neighbor. People changed it to — love your neighbor and hate your enemy. But I say to you that you are to love your enemies."
                                                        - Jesus, Matthew 5:43-44

Jesus spoke with an authority that only God possesses. Jesus said, "But I say to you" in these verses: Matthew 5:21-22; 27-28; 31-32; 33-34; 38-39; 43-44

Can a created being say what Jesus said?

Jesus said:

> "The heavens and the earth will pass away:
>   but My words will never pass away."
> Mark 13:31

Jesus called God's words "My words." Jesus said it again in John 8:31. He said, "If you continue in My Word, then you are My true disciples."

When the prophets spoke, God was speaking His words through them. The prophets never called God's words their own words. They never said, "My words."

Only God Himself could say what Jesus said. Michael the archangel would never commit an offense by saying the things that only God can say. Only Jesus can call God's word's "My words" because only Jesus is God.

Yes. Jehovah said this to Jesus:

> "Your throne, Oh God, is for ever and ever."   Hebrews 1:8

Hebrews 1:8 says that that's Jehovah calling Jesus God.

(See Psalms: 45:6)

What did Jesus ask the Pharisees?

The Pharisees were fake religious leaders who had seized control of the religious institutions. They put their <u>own</u> teachings alongside God's teachings and forced the people to follow them. They saw Jesus as a threat to their authority because Jesus freed the people from their cruelty.   (See Mark 7:1-23 and Matthew 15:20)

The Pharisees <u>did</u> know the Bible though. They knew the Bible predicted that <u>their Savior</u>, called the Christ (or Messiah, in Hebrew), would be a descendant of David, the king of Israel.

(See 2 Samuel 7:8-29; Psalms 132:11; Isaiah 11:1,10,
Jesse was David's father;
Ezekiel 34:23-25,29; 37:24-25, Sometimes the Old Testament says
"David" when it's talking about Jesus;
Also see Matthew 1:1; Revelation 5:5; 22:16)

Jesus is <u>that Savior</u>. Jesus is the Christ. That's why Jesus is called <u>the</u> Son of David. But the Pharisees hated Jesus and rejected the idea that Jesus was the Christ.

> Jesus used the Bible and sharp-as-a-tack thinking to box His enemies into a corner. One day Jesus challenged the Pharisees to solve a puzzle:

Jesus said:

> "I want to know your thoughts about the Christ:
>   whose Son is He?"   - Jesus, Matthew 22:42

The Pharisees answered:

"The Son of David."   Matthew 22:42

Then Jesus said to them:

"You're right, the Messiah is the son of David. But I'd like you to explain something to Me. King David wrote Psalms 110:1 through the direction of God's Holy Spirit.

And in that verse David wrote this about the Messiah: 'Jehovah said to my Lord,"Sit at My right hand until I make Your enemies Your footstool."'

If the Messiah is the son of David then why did David call the Messiah Lord?"   - Jesus, Matthew 22:43-45

Up to this point the Pharisees would sometimes make believe they respected Jesus as a teacher and ask Him questions about the Bible. The Pharisees thought they were the smart ones. They thought they could trick Jesus with their phony questions.   (See John 8:1-6)

But guess what? Jesus silenced the Pharisees. His question about the Son of David got them. None of them were able to answer His question. They didn't like His question. And from that point on the Pharisees were too scared to ask Jesus any more questions.

But, do you know who loved the question Jesus asked about the Son of David? The great crowd of people who were listening as Jesus talked with the Pharisees loved it. They loved it so much that they wanted to hear everything Jesus was saying.   (Mark 12:37)
(Matthew 22:41-46; Mark 12:35-37; Luke 20:41-44)

"The Lord said to my Lord." What does that mean? It means that Jehovah called Jesus God. It means Jesus is God. Why else would Jesus ask the Pharisees that question? Jesus asked it to force the Pharisees to either admit that Jesus is God or shut their mouths.

Has anyone seen Jehovah?

Yes, people saw Jehovah when they saw Jesus:

On the night before Jesus was to be crucified, one of His apostles, named Philip, said to Jesus,

"Lord, show us Jehovah."   John 14:8

And Jesus said:

"How is it Philip, that after I've been with you now for such a long time that you still don't know Me? Whoever has seen Me has seen Jehovah."   - Jesus, John 14:9

What happened before Jesus came to us?
First Timothy 6:16 says that no one has seen God, and no one can, because God lives in light which no human being can come near to.
                                (See Psalms 104:1-2)

God came down to Mount Sinai to give the 10 Commandments to the children of Israel. God told them that if they touched the mountain while He was there then they would die. The one exception was Moses.
                                (Exodus 19:12-13,20-25)

God came down in fire. The mountain shook violently. There was thunder, lightning, and smoke like a furnace.

After hearing God speak, the children of Israel told Moses they wanted <u>him</u> to speak to them instead. They said they were afraid that if God spoke to them again that they would die.   (Exodus 20:18-19)

But Moses told the people,

"Don't be afraid. God did this to find out if you would stay faithful to Him, and to put in your face a reason to fear Him, so that you will not sin."   Exodus 20:20

Later on, Moses told the children of Israel,

"When we were at Mount Sinai, God spoke to me and told me that He was happy to hear what you said. God said He will give you everything you asked for when you asked to not see the great fire anymore and not hear His voice anymore so that you don't die.

God will raise up a Prophet. He will be a flesh and blood human being like me, a member of your family. Obey Him.

God will speak His words from that Prophet's mouth. He will speak everything that God commands Him to speak.

And God said this: 'If anyone does not obey My words which that Prophet will speak in My name, then I will judge that person.'"
Deuteronomy 18:15-19
(See also Matthew 17:5-7; John 1:21; 5:46; 6:14)

That Prophet is Jesus, the Word of God.

The apostle John wrote:

"The Word of God entered a human body and walked among us. We saw His glory. It is a glory exactly like the glory of the only one who is God's own Son. And in Him is all of God's grace and truth."
John 1:14

"No human eyes have ever seen God. But the only begotten Son, who was in the bosom of the Father, He has revealed God to us."
John 1:18

God is so holy that if we were in His presence we would become so aware of our sinful filthiness that we would probably burst into flames. But if we believe in Jesus, then we will go to God in peace. He will receive us.   (See John 12:44-50)

"Happiness is overflowing out of those who are pure in heart,
  because they will see Jehovah."   - Jesus, Matthew 5:8

Who is worshiped as God?

The devil said to Jesus:

"Fall down and worship me."   - the devil, Matthew 4:9

The devil asked Jesus to worship him as though the devil was God. How do I know that? Because Jesus said this to the devil:

"It is written, 'Worship Jehovah, your God, and don't worship anyone else other than Him.'"   - Jesus, Matthew 4:10
(See Deuteronomy 6:13; 10:20)

> Jesus said that only God is to be worshiped, and no one else is to be worshiped as God.

Did people worship Jesus?
Yes, they did. When Jesus was resurrected from the dead, He went to Mary Magdalene and another woman named Mary who were walking down the road.

When those two women saw Jesus, they fell down before Him, put their hands on His feet and held them like they would never let go. And they worshiped Jesus.   (Matthew 28:9)

In what way did people worship Jesus?
Now, someone might tell you that the women weren't worshiping Jesus as God, that they were just showing respect like a student would show respect to a human teacher or to a human who is in a position of authority over them.

Can we find an example of that kind of worship?
Yes. Jesus told a story that teaches us the importance of forgiving people. In the story, a man who was a servant of a certain king owed the king a lot of money, and the king told the man to pay up now, or else.   (See Matthew 18:21-35)

Then the man fell down and worshiped the king, and said, lord, have patience with me, and I will pay back everything I owe you.

Now we're going to use the three steps to understanding that I told you about in chapter two of this book (page 24).

The first step: Original languages

The first step is looking at the meaning of words in the original languages. Take your Strong's Concordance and look up the words "worship" and "worshiped." The Strong's shows you every verse in the New Testament where those words are used. After each verse you see a number.

You use that number to find the word in the Greek dictionary in the back of the Strong's. The numbers from the Strong's are also used in other Greek dictionaries, like the one by Spiros Zodhiates, which gives much more in-depth definitions than the Strong's does.

Here's what we find

In Matthew 18:26, where we read that the servant worshiped the king he owed money to, the word "worshiped" is #4352.

Here's where it gets interesting

We just read Matthew 4:10, where Jesus told the devil that the Old Testament said, "Worship Jehovah, your God." Can you guess what number the word "worship" is in this verse? It's also #4352.

The second step: Context

When the servant showed respect to the king, a human being, the word 'worship" is #4352; and when Jesus said "worship Jehovah," the word for "worship" is also #4352. Now we need the second step: context. Who is speaking? Who are they speaking to? What was said before and after? What does it mean to us when we consider everything else that the Bible is teaching us?

I said before that context trumps word meanings. Why? Because the meaning of words can change. We see that in this example. The same word that is used for worshiping God is also used for showing respect to a human authority. Remember our Guide. Do the math.

Jesus said, Worship (#4352) Jehovah. We know that Jehovah is God, so we know that in this case # 4352 means to worship God. And we know that the king was a man. So when the servant worshiped (#4352) the king, he was showing respect to a human authority, not worshiping him as God.

This is why we have to study and think. Yes! <u>You</u> must do that. I know, some churches will make you think you shouldn't study or think. But you have to answer to God for what you did for Him. You can't let your church do your studying or thinking. And they can't speak to God for you. In the end, it's you and God.

So, what about Jesus?
We know that Jesus is God. The Bible says so. Jesus Himself said so. That's our context. There were certainly some people who didn't know Jesus was God and worshiped Him in the sense of showing respect to a human teacher. But those who know that Jesus is God worship Him as God.

The third step: God-given understanding
Why can't some people see that Jesus is God? Because they haven't been given that understanding by God. Why not? Well, one reason could be that they're listening to a man to the point where they've refused to listen to God.   (Please see 2 Timothy 4:3-4)

You'll never understand if you only have the first two steps. Only those who have the third step can see Jesus. And only believers have the third step.   (See Psalms 127:1)

Is Jesus worshiped as God?

Only Jehovah and Jesus are to be worshiped as God because Jesus is Jehovah and Jehovah is God. In Revelation chapters 4 and 5, we see both Jehovah and Jesus worshiped as God.

• Revelation 4:8-11 tells us about how **Jehovah** is worshiped:

"The four living creatures do not rest. All day and night they are saying, 'Holy, holy, holy, Jehovah God Almighty, who was, and is, and is to come.'

"And when those four living ones give glory and honor and thanks to the One sitting on the throne, the One who lives forever and ever, the twenty four elders fall down and worship Him who lives forever and ever, and cast their crowns before His throne.

And they say, 'You are worthy, Oh Jehovah, our Lord, to take hold of glory and honor and power.'"

Revelation 4:8-11

• Revelation 5:7-8,11-14 tells us about how **Jesus** is worshiped:

"When the Lamb, Jesus, took the book from the right hand of Him who sat on the throne, the twenty four elders fell down before the Lamb. Every one of them had a harp, and gold bowls full of incense, which symbolize the prayers of the believers.

And I, John, looked, and I heard the voice of many angels round about the throne and the four living creatures, and the elders. And there were so many of them that they could not be counted.

And they all said with a loud voice, 'Worthy is the Lamb, Jesus, who was killed, to take hold of power, and riches, and wisdom, and strength, and honor, and glory, and blessing.'

And every created being in Heaven, and on earth, and in the place of the dead, and on the sea, I heard them all saying, 'Blessing, and honor, and glory, and power, to Jehovah, the One Who sits on the throne, and to the Lamb, Jesus, for ever and ever.

And the four living creatures said 'Amen.' And they worshiped."

Revelation 5:7-8,11-14   (See Revelation 7:9-12)

They worshiped Jehovah and Jesus. The same worship was given to both. Jesus said, "Jehovah and Me are one."   (John 10:30)

When the apostles asked Jesus to pray, Jesus said, "When you pray, say, 'Our Father, who is in Heaven.'" But we just read in Revelation 5:8 that the twenty four elders bring the prayers of the believers to Jesus.

(See Luke 11:1-3)

Who else worshiped Jesus as God?

In John chapter 9, Jesus gave sight to a man who had been blind from birth. After Jesus gave the man sight, Jesus said to him, "Surely, now, after that, you must be a believer in the Son of God." And the man said, "Tell me who He is Lord, so I can believe in Him." Jesus said, "You've seen Him, and He is speaking with you right now." The man said, "Lord, I believe." And then the man worshiped Jesus.

(John 9:38)

There's so much there. The man worshiped the Son of God. We know that "the Son of God" means that Jesus is 100% God. People wanted to kill Jesus for calling God His own Father. The man received eternal life by believing in Jesus, the Son of God, who is 100% God.

Only Jehovah is the Savior. Jesus is Jehovah.   (See Isaiah 45:21-22)

The apostles worshiped Jesus as God

When the apostles got caught in a storm at sea, Jesus walked to them on the water. Then Jesus got in the boat with them and the storm stopped. Here's what happened next:

"Then they who were in the boat worshiped Jesus, and said, 'You truly are God's own Son.'"   Matthew 14:33

Here's what happened when Jesus went back to Heaven:

"Jesus had His disciples walk with Him until they reached the town of Bethany. Then Jesus lifted up His hands and blessed the disciples.

While Jesus was blessing the disciples He went and stood by Himself. Then Jesus was carried up into Heaven.

And the disciples worshiped Jesus.

Then the disciples returned to Jerusalem filled with great joy. And they would go to the temple when the people were meeting there, and they would sing about the greatness of God and speak good things about God."

Luke 24:50-53

The men who crucified Jesus did this to Him:

> "They kept on hitting Jesus and spitting on Him. And they bowed their knees to Jesus and worshiped Him." Mark 15:19

The word "worshiped" here is once again #4352. Remember? That's the same word Jesus used in Matthew 4:10, when He said "worship Jehovah." But the next verse tells us that those men weren't worshiping Jesus as God — they were laughing at Jesus. The same word that Jesus used for worshiping Jehovah is used here for the fake worship those men gave to Jesus. (Mark 15:20)

The word "Lord"

The way the word "Lord" is used in the Bible forces us to study and think. Yes, God wants you to think. You'll never understand the Bible if you don't think — your own thinking, not some man's thoughts.

The Greek word that is translated into English as "Lord" is #2962. The meaning of the word changes according to the context in which it's used. It can be a term of respect used when speaking to a human authority or it can be used when speaking to God.

In Matthew 13:27 ("sir") and 1 Peter 3:6 ("lord"), the Greek word #2962 is used to show respect to human beings.

Jesus said this to His apostles:

> "When you speak to Me, you call Me Teacher and Lord. You got that right. Because I am." - Jesus, John 13:13

What did the apostle Thomas say?

> "Jesus said to Thomas, 'Look at My hands. Go ahead, use your finger. Now take your hand and put it in My side. Stop doubting that I rose from the dead, and start believing!'"
>
> - Jesus, John 20:27

> "And Thomas said to Jesus, 'My Lord and my God.'" John 20:28

When <u>humans</u> were called "sir" and "lord," the word used is #2962. When Jesus and Thomas called <u>Jesus</u> "Lord," the word is #2962. Context makes the difference.

Is Jesus the archangel Michael?

In the Book of Revelation, the apostle John fell down at the feet of an angel to worship him, but the angel said to John:

"Don't do that. I'm a fellow servant, like you and the others who are witnesses for Jesus, and all those who guard the words of the Bible. Worship God."   Revelation 22:8-9

The word "archangel" simply means a high-ranking angel. The archangel Michael is an angel, nothing more. John was told by an angel <u>not</u> to worship <u>him</u>, but to only worship <u>God</u>.   (See Acts 10:25-26; 14:11-15; Col.2:18; Heb 1:6)

The Jehovah's Witnesses say that Jesus is the archangel Michael. But Jesus <u>never</u> said what the angel said to John when John tried to worship that angel. When Mary Magdalene and the other Mary, and the apostles, and the blind man worshiped Jesus, Jesus didn't stop them and tell them to worship God. Why? Because Jesus <u>is</u> God!

Did Jesus say that people would be worshiped?

Jesus told the believers of the church in Philadelphia that He would make those who were only pretending to be believers come and worship before their feet. Once again, the Greek word for "worship" used here is #4352, the same word that Jesus used when He said to worship Jehovah in Matthew 4:10. So what did Jesus mean here?

(Revelation 3:9)

Let's go to the Old Testament

Nebuchadnezzar, the king of Babylon, had a dream one night, and none of his people could figure out the meaning of the dream.

(Daniel 2:1-18)

But there was an Israelite named Daniel who was being held in Babylon. God revealed to Daniel the meaning of Nebuchadnezzar's dream. (Daniel 2:19-45)

Here's what happened when Daniel told Nebuchadnezzar that God had revealed to him the meaning of the dream:

"Nebuchadnezzar fell upon his face, and worshiped Daniel."
Daniel 2:46

Did Nebuchadnezzar worship Daniel?

No, he did not. How do I know? Because Daniel was a good man. And Daniel did not say to Nebuchadnezzar, "Don't do that, worship God." (Daniel 2:48)

Daniel let Nebuchadnezzar do what he did because Nebuchadnezzar wasn't worshiping Daniel. He was worshiping Daniel's God. (Daniel 2:47)

And when Jesus said He will make certain people come and worship at the feet of the believers of the church in Philadelphia, Jesus did not mean they would be worshiping the believers but that they would be worshiping the believer's God.

Believers stand in front of God, like children in front of their loving parents.

Chapter nine

Is the Holy Spirit
a person?

The Jehovah's Witnesses tell people that the Holy Spirit is not a person. They are wrong. God has given us the proof to teach us who the Holy Spirit is.

Is Jehovah a person?

Jesus said this:

"If anyone loves Me, then they will show that they love Me. They will show their love for Me, first, by listening carefully to what I say. They will cherish My words, guard them, and protect them.

And, they will obey Me, they will do what I tell them to do.

Jehovah will love them for doing that. And because they do that, Me and Jehovah will come to them. And we will make our home in that person's heart."   - Jesus, John 14:23

Jesus said that He and Jehovah will live in believer's hearts. That's the Holy Spirit. But the Jehovah's Witnesses say that the Holy Spirit is not a person.

So what the Jehovah's Witnesses are saying then is that Jehovah is not a person, and that Jesus is not a person.

Is Jesus zero percent God?

The Jehovah's Witnesses teach that Jesus was created by Jehovah. They make Jesus zero percent God. But Jesus said that He and Jehovah will make their home in believer's hearts.

The Jehovah's Witnesses want you to believe that Jehovah will take someone with Him who is zero percent God, to live in the hearts of believers. There's no such thing. Only God can live in the hearts of believers. That means that in John 14:23, Jesus said that He is God.

Are the Jehovah's Witnesses Christians?

(I'll tell you on page 102)

Here's what the apostle Paul wrote:

"If anyone does not have the Spirit of Christ, then they do not belong to Christ."   Romans 8:9

"Here's how we know that we will live with God forever: We know because God has given us His Holy Spirit.

God let us understand something, and we explain it to others. It is this: Jehovah sent Jesus, and Jesus is the Savior of the world.

If anyone agrees with us that Jesus is God's own Son, it means that God has made His home in that person's heart, and that person will live forever."   1 John 4:13-15

Why don't the Jehovah's Witnesses love Jehovah?

Jesus said this:

"Jehovah gave you plenty of evidence that He sent Me. But you never wanted to see it. You never wanted to see Jehovah.

You do not have Jehovah's Word living in your hearts and minds because you refuse to believe in the One Jehovah sent.

I know you. And I know that you do not love Jehovah. I came to you in Jehovah's name and you wouldn't receive Me.

There's someone else who will come to you in his own name, and you will receive him."   - Jesus, John 5:37-38,42-43

Let's review the evidence
• The apostle John wrote that Jehovah will make His home in the hearts of those who agree that Jesus is Jehovah's own Son.

• The Jehovah's Witnesses do not agree with that, so Jehovah will not make His home in their hearts.

• The apostle Paul wrote that those who do not have the Spirit of Christ, the Holy Spirit, do not belong to Christ.

The Jehovah's Witnesses do not have the Holy Spirit. And besides, the Jehovah's Witnesses say that the Holy Spirit is not even a person. Therefore, they are rejecting Jehovah and Jesus.

Jesus said that people who refuse to believe that He is God's own Son, do that because they don't love Jehovah. Jesus said they don't have God's true Word living in them. When Jesus said they will receive someone else, He was talking about the Antichrist.

Do you know what the name "Antichrist"means? It means "instead of Christ." And do you know who the Antichrist is? He is the devil.

The Jehovah's Witnesses have rejected Jesus and received the devil. The Jehovah's Witnesses have rejected God's Holy Spirit, and have instead received the spirit of the Antichrist. They don't belong to Christ. They belong to the devil.

They have rejected God's Word and received a lie. That's why they won't receive Jesus. They received a counterfeit Jesus instead. So, no, the Jehovah's Witnesses are not Christians. They are fake Christians, impostors.

Are the Jehovah's Witnesses going to Heaven?

No, the Jehovah's Witnesses are not going to Heaven. Who am I to say that? I didn't say it. Jesus did. Jesus said that if a person has not been given a second birth by the Holy Spirit, then they will never enter Heaven, and they won't even ever see Heaven.   (See John 3:1-8)

The Jehovah's Witnesses can't go to Heaven. They're not born again. They're committing the same sin as the scribes and Pharisees, and others who also spoke evil about and rejected God's Holy Spirit.
                    (Matthew 12:24-34; Mark 3:21-30; Luke 11:14-15)

Is the Holy Spirit a person?

On the night before He was crucified, Jesus met with His apostles. He had much to teach them in their last hours together. Jesus knew He would die, then rise from death, and then go back to Heaven.

So, Jesus wanted to let the apostles know that He was not abandoning them, that He would be with them.

"If you love Me, then you will obey Me. Then Jehovah and Me will have a little talk about you. And after I go back to Heaven, then He will give you another Comforter who will never have to leave you.

I'm sending you away now. But you won't be by yourselves. I will come to you."
                                              - Jesus, John 14:15-16,18

Jesus is "another Comforter." Jesus said, "I will come back to you." First, Jesus came to them in a <u>human body</u>. But now that Jesus accomplished what He came to do, it's time for Him to leave and go back to Heaven. But Jesus will come back to the apostles, and all believers, in a way that He will never have to leave.

Jesus comes to us as the eternal Holy Spirit of God. Jesus is a person, so the Holy Spirit is a person.

Jesus is the Holy Spirit:

"The Lord (Jesus) is the Spirit."   2 Corinthians 3:17

Jehovah is the Holy Spirit:

The apostle Peter accused a man named Ananias of lying to the Holy Spirit (Acts 5:3). And in the next verse, Peter told Ananias that he lied to God (Acts 5:4).

The Holy Spirit has feelings

"Jehovah's people rebelled against Him and made His Holy Spirit's heart ache. They made Jehovah their enemy, and He fought against them."   Isaiah 63:10

King David wrote this to Jehovah:

"There's no place that I can go to hide from Your Spirit; there's nowhere I can go to flee from Your presence."   Psalms 139:7

Jesus said this:

"If someone holds on tightly to My words and never lets go, and obeys what I say, then that is the person who loves Me. And if someone loves Me, then Jehovah will love them. And I will love them, and I will let them see Me."   - Jesus, John 14:21

When Jesus says He will let those who love Him see Him, Jesus means that He will let them understand Him, as a close friend. They will see Jesus clearly. And, it's a kind of seeing that no one can do on their own. It's a kind of understanding that no one can get on their own.

(See John 15:14)

The only ones who can see Jesus that way are the ones that Jesus lets see Him that way. And Jesus only lets those who love Him see Him that way.

> That means the Jehovah's Witnesses are on the outside looking in. They hate Jesus. They go around telling lies about Him. So, Jesus won't come to them as the Holy Spirit. And they will never understand Jesus. He won't let them. The Jehovah's Witnesses can't see Jesus.

The Old Testament says:

"If they do not speak from God's Word it's because there is no light in them."   Isaiah 8:20

The Jehovah's Witnesses do not speak from God's Word. They speak lies. They reject Jesus, the Light of the world, and reject His Holy Spirit. There is no light in the Jehovah's Witnesses.   (See John 8:12)

Who says that Jesus is accursed?

The apostle Paul wrote:

"No one who has been given a new birth by God's Holy Spirit would ever go around telling people that Jesus is accursed.

And no one can call Jesus their Lord if they have not been given a new birth by God's Holy Spirit."   1 Corinthians 12:3

The King James Version says that no one speaking by God's Holy Spirit would ever call Jesus "accursed." Instead of "accursed" I'll say that the Jehovah's Witnesses call Jesus "the devil," like the other enemies of Jesus did. Those other enemies called Jesus the devil and called God's Holy Spirit the devil when they said that Jesus performed miracles by the power of the devil.   (Mark 3:22)

The Jehovah's Witnesses say Jesus was created by Jehovah. It was a created being called Lucifer who wanted to sit on God's throne. Lucifer became the devil. The Jehovah's Witnesses' Jesus is the devil.
                                    (See Isaiah 14:12-17; Ezekiel 28:11-19)

The Jehovah's Witnesses want to put a created being where only God can sit. They're calling Jesus the devil, or accursed, or however you want to say it. And they do that because they reject God's Holy Spirit by saying His Holy Spirit is not a person.   (Matthew 22:44; 26:64)

> The apostle Paul wrote that those who do not have the Holy Spirit cannot call Jesus their Lord. The Jehovah's Witnesses will never call Jesus their Lord because they don't have the Holy Spirit. Therefore, the Jehovah's Witnesses are doomed.   (1 Corinthians 12:3)

Who does understand?

The apostle John wrote:

"You have been given a special oil from the Holy One. That's why you understand these things."   1 John 2:20

That special oil is God's Holy Spirit. You'll never know God unless He gives you that special oil.

Who can't be fooled by the Jehovah's Witnesses?

"I've written this letter to warn you about people who are trying to pull you away from Jesus.

But the special oil that you were given by Him lives inside you, so you don't need people to teach you."   1 John 2:26-27

(See John 6:45)

Human teachers are good. The point John is making is that when God gives you His Holy Spirit then God becomes your teacher, and you're not going to be fooled by people like the Jehovah's Witnesses. They can't pull you away from Jesus.

(See Ephesians 4:11-13)

How do you test the Jehovah's Witnesses?

The apostle John wrote:

"I write this to you who are dear to God's heart. I need to tell you something urgently important. It is this: Someone might claim to be teaching truths from the Bible, but they might not have the Holy Spirit of God. So, don't just believe what every Bible teacher says to you.

You've got to test what they teach. Their teachings might be from God. Or they might be from evil spirits, and from the devil. I have to tell you this because there are many people who are teaching lies, and claiming that those lies are the true teachings of God.

Here's how you know if a teacher has God's Holy Spirit: If they teach that Jehovah our Savior came and lived in a human body, then that teacher is from God.

And if they do not teach that Jehovah our Savior came and lived in a human body, then that teacher is not from God, they have the spirit of the Antichrist.

You've heard from myself and other Christian teachers that the spirit of the Antichrist would come, and it is already here."

1 John 4:1-3

The name "Jesus" means "Jehovah our Savior." Jesus is Jehovah our Savior. John is warning us that there are people who are setting themselves up as Bible teachers, and who claim to be teaching truth from the Bible. But they do not teach that Jesus is Jehovah our Savior, who came from Heaven and lived in a human body.

They teach that Jesus is someone else. They teach that Jesus was created by Jehovah, or that Jesus is the archangel Michael. They teach that Jesus is zero percent God.

John's not saying that those who do teach that Jehovah lived in a human body never make any mistakes. Jesus was the only perfect person. And yes, there might be teachers who say the words "Jehovah our Savior came and lived in a flesh body" but are false teachers because they don't really believe it.

John is making a point about people who have crossed a certain line, and that makes them servants of the devil.

The Antichrist hasn't come yet. That will happen later. The devil is powerful, and his evil spirit, the spirit of Antichrist, is working in the world now to pull people away from Jesus.   (1 John 2:18)

How do you deal with the Jehovah's Witnesses?

The apostle John told us what to do:

"There are people who are setting themselves up as though they are some great Bible teachers. But they <u>do not</u> have Jehovah.

What's flowing through their veins is something very different than the true teachings about Jesus that you received from Jesus Himself and from His apostles.

But those Bible teachers who <u>do</u> have the true teachings about Jesus flowing through their veins <u>do</u> have Jehovah, because they have both Jehovah and Jesus.

Now if any of those so-called Bible teachers come to you, the ones who don't have Jesus or Jehovah, then <u>do not</u> welcome them into your house. And don't say to them, 'Be happy.'

Because if you say to them, 'Be happy,' then you become a partner with them in their deadly work."   2 John 1:9-11

Chapter ten

Conclusion

Can you be fooled by
the <u>artificial</u> logic of the Jehovah's Witnesses?

On their website, JW.org, the Jehovah Witnesses make an appeal to logic. <u>They</u> say that logic suggests that Jesus <u>can't</u> be <u>both</u> God <u>and</u> the Son of God.

The Jehovah's Witnesses have a lot of booklets filled with arguments that <u>sound</u> convincing. They tell you that the idea of "the trinity" comes from pagan religions, and show you a picture of what looks like a three-headed god.

They're right. The trinity <u>is</u> a pagan concoction. So, people might say, "Hey, those Jehovah's Witnesses are pretty smart." Yes, the Jehovah's Witnesses have presented you with a truth. But why? Because now they've won you, they've convinced you that they are true teachers. You've taken the bait. And now they can trick you.

How do they do that? By working off of the truth they gave you. Now they take the next step. <u>They</u> say that because the trinity is a false teaching of pagan religions, then therefore only Jehovah can be God <u>and</u> therefore Jesus <u>can't</u> be God, and the Holy Spirit is <u>not</u> a person.

What the Jehovah's Witnesses are using to trick people is <u>artificial</u> logic. Suppose you're standing at a distance from artificial flowers. They appear to be real flowers. You can't tell that they're artificial until you look closely and handle them. Then you see that there's no life in them, they're dead.

The logic of the Jehovah's Witnesses is plastic. It's man-made. It only has the appearance of being real, but it's not real. It's bogus. Why is that? Because Jesus is "the Logos" (the original Greek for "the Word" in John 1:1). The Logos is logic. Jesus is logic. And logic is <u>truth</u>. You can't have logic without truth. Truth is found in the Holy Bible. The truth found in the Bible is that Jesus <u>is</u> both God and the Son of God.

The so-called logic of the Jehovah's Witnesses might <u>sound</u> right, it might <u>seem</u> to be correct. But it's only when you dig deeper that you see what's really going on.

The Jehovah's Witnesses are stealing from God.

- They're stealing God's <u>love</u>

They're taking away from God the great love that He feels for every person. How are they doing that? They do that by teaching that some created being, some thing, died on the cross. No, it was not some freak of nature that was created by the Jehovah's Witnesses who died on the cross.

<u>God</u> did that for us. Don't take that from Him. God gets all the glory, all the credit. You're stealing God's glory and God's love for us. God so loved the world that He gave His Son. God did that. He did it. God didn't send an angel or some Frankenstein monster to die on the cross.

(John 3:16; 1 John 4:9-10)

Get to know God

I showed you how the meaning of words in the Bible can change depending on their context. That leaves plenty of room for deceivers to do their work — deceivers exploit context. We have to cultivate our relationship with God by studying the Bible. It's up to us to get to know our Guide so we can stay on the right path and know God. Enjoy these:

"They have no reason to hate Me. I don't deserve their hatred."
- Jesus, John 15:25

"Here's the truth: I honor Jehovah, and you dishonor Me."
- Jesus, John 8:49

"Jehovah wants everyone to honor His Son in the same way that they honor Him. Anyone who does not honor the Son, does not honor Jehovah, the One who sent the Son."
- Jesus, John 5:23

"Whoever strips Me of My rank, strips Jehovah of His rank."
- Jesus, Luke 10:16

The apostle Paul wrote this:

"If the Gospel has been hidden, it is hidden from those who are lost because they don't believe.

And because they don't believe, then they've let the god of <u>this world</u> blind their minds, so that the glorious Gospel of Christ — Who is the exact image of God — is not understood by them.

I, Paul, am your servant. I serve you because of Jesus. I don't preach myself to you. I preach Christ Jesus as Lord.

Because God, the One who, back in Genesis, commanded the light to shine out of the darkness, has shined in our hearts, to give us the light of the glory of God in <u>the face</u> of Jesus Christ."

2 Corinthians 4:3-6

Who is "the god of this world?" It's the devil. See, what happened? The Jehovah's Witnesses called Jesus "a god." But the god that the Jehovah's Witnesses are serving is the devil.

You cannot trust Bible teachers who don't have the Holy Spirit.

True believers worship Jesus as Lord. And God rewards us by uncovering our minds, and shining His light in our hearts, so that when we see the face of Jesus we know that we are seeing the glory of God.

(See John 1:18; 2:11; 6:45-48; Colossians 2:3; Hebrews 1:3)

"Jesus is an <u>exact</u> picture of God." - 2 Corinthians 4:4

"You are of God, little children. And you have overcome the false teachers who have the spirit of the Antichrist because Jehovah lives in you. And Jehovah is greater than the spirit of the Antichrist that lives in the world."
1 John 4:4

What are the last words in the Bible?

The very last verse in the Bible is this:

> "The grace of our Lord Jesus be with all of you who believe."
> Revelation 22:21

The last verse of the Bible is about the Lord Jesus. Would God end the Bible with a verse about Michael the archangel, or some other created being? No, of course not. God ended the Bible with a verse about the Lord Jesus.

And it says, "the grace of our Lord Jesus." That's God's grace, not the grace of Michael or any other created being.

Grace is the gift that God gives to His people. Only God gives that grace which saves a person's soul. Ephesians 2:8 says that we are saved because of God's grace, and that grace is a gift that God gives us.

You can read about the grace of our Lord Jesus in Psalms 45:2, and the grace of Jehovah in Genesis 39:21. That is the same grace.

> "I am the Way, and the Truth, and the Life."
> - Jesus, John 14:6

Will the Jehovah's Witnesses change their mind now?

So, the Jehovah's Witnesses should be changing their minds now after they read this book, right? Wrong. Why not? Well, one reason is that they won't read this book.

Cults instill <u>fear</u> in their people. They rule their people with an iron fist. People in cults are afraid to think for themselves. Because if they do, then they will be subjected to bitterness and ridicule.

There's a woman I know. She's in her mid-seventies. She has the discernment of a baby. English is not her first language. She has become a victim of the Jehovah's Witnesses.

At one point I convinced her to throw out all of her Jehovah's Witnesses books. But the Jehovah's Witnesses pursued her relentlessly. They took advantage of her weakness, her loneliness, and her fear of them. They would sneak into her building and knock on her door.

I was actually with this woman in her apartment once when two Jehovah's Witnesses showed up unannounced. When I told the woman she shouldn't have let them in her apartment, the Jehovah's Witnesses became angry. They snapped at me, "Are you her husband?"

People in cults are vicious and cruel — wolves in sheep's clothing. They have no compassion, no mercy. The Jehovah's Witnesses succeeded in getting the woman back into their clutches. They don't care that the woman doesn't even understand what the Jehovah's Witnesses are about. She's just another number to them.

Later on I offered the woman a copy of my book, AHA moments from the Bible. But she refused to take it. Of course not. Thinking for yourself is forbidden in cults.

If you follow a man or a cult then you will prefer <u>them</u> over God. You'll choose <u>their</u> influence instead of the Holy Spirit. You'll be taught by men instead of God and you'll be swimming in lies.

Who gets the glory?

All the glory goes to God. I thank God for giving me His Word and His Holy Spirit. I'm a filthy sinner, but God picked me up out of the sewer and gave me a ministry. And now, all I want to do is work for Him and use what He gives me to show people His Word, the Bible.

Do you know how much I appreciate you?

And I thank God for giving me the few fellow Christians who appreciate my ministry. When I study the Bible I'm always thinking about you, looking for things I can share with you, and looking forward to feeding you the Word of God, because you're the ones who love the Word. You know who you are.

I thoroughly enjoyed writing this book for you. It brought me on a great adventure of Bible study. That's my happy place. The only thing I've enjoyed more than studying the Bible by myself was being in the Word with people on the street corner. I thank all of you who loved to be in the Word with me on the street corner.

To my best friend. Thank you. You've always been cheerfully willing to do whatever was needed for the ministry. I know. And I hope you know how much I appreciate you.

"How do we learn what true love is? Jesus showed us what true love is when He laid down His life for us. We owe it to Jesus to do the same, by laying down our life for our brothers and sisters."
1 John 3:16

Dear reader: Please let me know what conclusion you've come to. Bruce Benson   heartwishbooks@gmail.com

Who's Number One?

Jesus is. Jesus is the Greatest. Jesus is Numero Uno.

"I am the Truth" - Jesus, John 14:6

"When the Spirit of Truth comes,
He will Guide you to all the truth."
- Jesus, John 16:13

CPSIA information can be obtained
at www.ICGtesting.com
Printed in the USA
LVHW091446250520
656547LV00002B/831